CONTRACTING FOR PROPERTY RIGHTS

POLITICAL ECONOMY OF INSTITUTIONS AND DECISIONS

editors
Professor James Alt, Washington University in St. Louis
Professor Douglass North, Washington University in St. Louis

Other books in the series

Yoram Barzel, *Economic Analysis of Property Rights*

Robert H. Bates, *Beyond the Miracle of the Market: The Politics of Agrarian Development in Kenya*

Gary W. Cox, *The Efficient Secret*

Mathew D. McCubbins and Terry Sullivan (eds.), *Congress Structure and Policy*

Charles Stewart III, *Budget Reform Politics: The Design of the Appropriations Process in the House of Representatives, 1865–1921*

CONTRACTING FOR PROPERTY RIGHTS

GARY D. LIBECAP

Published by the Press Syndicate of the University of Cambridge
The Pitt Building, Trumpington Street, Cambridge CB2 1RP
40 West 20th Street, New York, NY 10011-4211, USA
10 Stamford Road, Oakleigh, Melbourne 3166, Australia

First published 1989
First paperback edition 1993

Printed in the United States of America

Library of Congress Cataloging-in-Publication Data available.

A catalogue record for this book is available from the British Library.

ISBN 0-521-36620-8 hardback
ISBN 0-521-44904-9 paperback

For Ann, Sarah, and Cap

Contents

Series Editors' Preface

The Cambridge series in the Political Economy of Institutions and Decisions is built around attempts to answer two central questions: How do institutions evolve in response to individual incentives, strategies, and choices? How do institutions affect the performance of political and economic systems? The scope of the series is comparative and historical rather than international or specifically American, and the focus is positive rather than normative.

Gary Libecap's *Contracting for Property Rights* is a study of the way property rights institutions are formed. The very substantial literature on these economic institutions has made abundantly clear that property rights matter; that they provide the basic incentive system that shapes resource allocation. What has been largely missing is why they take the form that they do. Why do some property rights structures lead to productive activity and underpin economic growth, while others result in waste and unproductive activity? Libecap's study emphasizes that property rights are formed and enforced by political entities and reflect the conflicting interests and bargaining strength of those affected. Moreover, because today's choices are constrained by yesterday's decisions, history matters.

Libecap's study is a synthesis of theory and history that illustrates and illumines the complexities of property rights formation in four natural resource industries in the American economy. These four empirical cases are contrasting studies of differential success in mitigating the losses from the common pool – losses that occurred even though in each case there were large aggregate gains to be made from reaching agreement. Libecap develops an analytical framework to account for these contrasting results. The result is a major contribution both to the theory of property rights formation and to our understanding of economic history.

1

Contracting for property rights

INTRODUCTION

Property rights are the social institutions that define or delimit the range of privileges granted to individuals to specific assets, such as parcels of land or water. Private ownership of these assets may involve a variety of rights, including the right to exclude nonowners from access, the right to appropriate the stream of rents from use of and investments in the resource, and the right to sell or otherwise transfer the resource to others. Property rights institutions range from formal arrangements, including constitutional provisions, statutes, and judicial rulings, to informal conventions and customs regarding the allocations and use of property. Such institutions critically affect decision making regarding resource use and, hence, affect economic behavior and performance. By allocating decision-making authority, they also determine who are the economic actors in a system and define the distribution of wealth in a society. Because of their important social role, property rights institutions have been the subject of attention by economists and economic historians, as well as by political scientists and sociologists. Surveys of the economics and economic history literature are provided by Furubotn and Pejovich (1972), North (1978), De Alessi (1980), and Libecap (1986). The focus of this literature largely has been on how various property rights arrangements affect behavior, which ranges from the wasteful practices associated with open-access or common pool settings to the wealth-maximizing actions possible with secure private property rights.

Because of the overwhelming advantages of secure property rights, economic agents often are hypothesized to adopt or to modify property

Acknowledgement: The author wishes to thank Anthony Scott for his careful reading of the manuscript and suggestions for change.

rights in order to mitigate the losses of the common pool, as soon as the private benefits of so doing outweigh the private costs. Forces that drive these adjustments in property rights include new market prices and production possibilities to which old arrangements are poorly attuned (Demsetz, 1967). Davis and North (1971, p. 39) are explicit in the argument: "It is the possibility of profits that cannot be captured within the existing arrangemental structure that leads to the formation of new (or the mutation of old) institutional arrangements." In other words, it is argued that market forces tend to erode property rights institutions that are ill suited for responding to new economic opportunities. If the existing rights structure limits or blocks reaction to changes in relative prices or technology, the existence of unexploited potential gains will lead individuals to adopt more accommodating property rights.

Despite these optimistic assertions in the literature, the actual process by which property institutions are changed and whether the changes represent an efficient solution to a particular social problem have received much less consideration. For example, a continuing puzzle is why we observe so much variety in the types of property institutions that exist. Some rights arrangements appear to be well structured to allocate resources to high-valued uses and to promote economic expansion, whereas others appear to limit decision flexibility and to instill incentives that retard economic growth. Moreover, historical studies of economic development reveal that differences in property rights institutions across societies with otherwise similar resource endowments have contributed importantly to observed variations in economic performance.

North and Thomas (1973) provide a case in point. They argue that the observed difference in growth rates in the sixteenth and seventeenth centuries between France and Spain, on the one hand, and England and the Netherlands, on the other, were due at least in part to differences in property rights arrangements. According to North and Thomas, in France and Spain absolutist monarchies relied on granting and taxing local monopoly privileges and were fearful of adjustments in property rights that might undermine their political and economic base, even if such changes offered broad economic gains. In England and the Netherlands, where commercial interests were politically stronger, property rights institutions tended to be adopted that allowed for more fluid resource movement to promote and to respond to growing markets.

Although closer examination of property rights in these four countries would be useful for evaluating the North and Thomas thesis, this case in European economic history, where property rights were maintained for distributional and political reasons at the expense of significantly greater economic growth, does not appear to be an isolated example. Indeed, North (1981, p. 6), as part of the progression of his thinking on this matter, noted: "But the fact that growth has been more exceptional than stagnation or decline suggests that efficient property rights are unusual in history."

The persistence of seemingly perverse property rights in the face of what would appear to be obvious alternatives recently has led to more attention to the origins of property institutions and to the process of institutional change. This concern with the underpinnings of property rights shares a common research agenda with a broader literature on institutional analysis.

One direction this literature has taken is an examination of the underlying reasons for the emergence of firms, rather than markets, to coordinate certain production activities. Beginning with Coase (1937) and including Alchian and Demsetz (1972), Jensen and Meckling (1976), Williamson (1981), and others, firms are viewed as developing as a means of reducing transactions costs in production and of diversifying risk. The adoption of institutions to reduce transactions costs is also the theme of related analyses of government regulation. Representative is the work of Goldberg (1976) and Williamson (1976), who argue that certain kinds of regulation, at least, can be interpreted as mechanisms for completing long-term contracts when private agreements are not forthcoming.

There are differences, though, between this institutional analysis literature and recent historical work on the development of property rights. As with earlier examinations of property rights, the institutional analysis literature tends to be the more optimistic one, viewing the design of various governance structures as maximizing decisions to economize on transactions costs. A problem with such claims, however, is the general failure to specify the size of the net benefits achieved from the adoption of a particular institutional form relative to the returns offered by its alternatives. This failure to identify the range of institutional options confronting decision makers and the likely costs and benefits associated with each one, makes it difficult to evaluate the maximization claims.

Regardless of whether observed institutions represent the most efficient responses to particular social and economic problems, both economic theory and history provide reasons for believing that the net social gains from changes in property rights at any time will be quite modest. This is because it is difficult to resolve the distributional conflicts inherent in major changes in ownership arrangements.[1] The nature of these conflicts and the problems they present for institutional change are the focus of this volume.[2]

THE IMPLICATIONS OF THEORY FOR SUCCESSFUL INSTITUTIONAL CHANGE

Throughout this volume, the term *contracting* is used to describe efforts by individuals to assign or to modify property rights. In this context, contracting includes bargaining among private claimants within groups to adopt or to change group rules and customs regarding the allocation and use of property. It also includes lobbying and political negotiations among private claimants, bureaucrats, politicians, and judges to implement or to alter more formal property laws and administrative rulings.

Because certain property rights arrangements can reduce transactions costs in exchange and production and encourage investment in order to promote overall economic growth, they have public goods aspects. As with all public goods, though, there are hazards in attempting to change in property rights. For example, there may be shirking and noncooperative behavior among the bargaining parties that will affect the institutions that can be established. In bargaining over creating or modifying property rights, the stands taken by the various bargaining parties, including private claimants, bureaucrats, and politicians, will be molded by their *private* expected gains, as well as by the actions of the other parties.[3]

Property rights institutions are determined through the political process, involving either negotiations among immediate group members or lobbying activities at higher levels of government. The political process of defining and enforcing property rights can be divisive because of the distributional implications of different property allocations. Although the aggregate gains from reducing common pool problems or from promoting economic growth through the definition or redefinition

[1]There are historical examples of changes in rights arrangements, such as the enclosure movement in England, that were accompanied by significant increases in the value of production (McCloskey, 1972). Nevertheless, the argument made here is that because of the complexity of contracting, most adjustments in property rights at any time will be quite limited in scope with various close alternatives possible. This points to the problems in developing a theory of institutional change that offers predictions regarding the particular type and impact of property rights that will be adopted.

[2]Successful institutional change is defined as changes in governance structures that promote economic growth.

[3]Binger and Hoffman (1989) rely upon the theory of repeated games and the existence of multiple Nash equilibria to argue that predictions regarding the development of particular institutions will be extremely difficult.

of property rights are unlikely to be controversial, the distribution of wealth and political power that are part of the transition to the proposed rights structure will be a source of dispute. In political bargaining over institutional change, each of the parties attempts to maximize his or her private net gains. These private net gains, which mold bargaining stands, are determined by the individual's anticipated share in the aggregate or social benefits resulting from modification in property rights institutions. However, both the aggregate benefits that are possible and the individual's position within them depend upon the share formula that is inherent in the proposed allocation of property.

In bargaining over changes in property rights, disagreements can occur over the nature of either the aggregate benefits or the shares, but the heart of the contracting problem is devising politically acceptable allocation mechanisms to assign the gains from institutional change while maintaining its production advantages. Because property rights involve the assignment of exclusive decision making over valuable resources, some parties will be harmed by the new definition of wealth and political power. Compensating those potentially harmed in the proposed definition of rights and increasing the shares of influential parties may produce a political consensus for institutional change. Those share concessions, however, necessarily alter the nature of the property rights under consideration and the size of the aggregate gains that are possible.

If influential parties cannot be sufficiently compensated through share adjustments in the political process to win their support, beneficial institutional change (even as modified through contracting concessions) may not occur, and the potential economic gains fostered by the proposed arrangement will be forgone. Even though society would be better off with the public goods provided by the new property rights, the distributional implications lead influential parties to oppose institutional change.[4] Accordingly, examination of the preferences of the individual bargaining parties and consideration of the details of the political bargaining underlying property rights institutions are necessary for understanding why particular property rights are developed and maintained, despite imaginable alternatives that would appear to be more rational.[5]

[4]Distributional concerns also appear as fairness considerations. For a discussion, see Hoffman and Spitzer (1985).

[5]For example, Libecap and Wiggins (1984) explain why prorationing was adopted in Oklahoma and Texas between 1926 and 1933 with individual production quotas that encouraged overdrilling. Although Adelman (1964) has criticized prorationing for leading to unnecessary wells, Libecap and Wiggins argue that per well quotas were adopted to build political consensus for prorationing. Although overdrilling resulted, prorationing provided some relief from common pool oil production.

In principle, it is possible to construct a side payment scheme that would compensate those who otherwise would oppose a desirable change in property rights. But in practice, the devising of perfectly compensating side payments to bring agreement encounters formidable obstacles, including questions of who should receive payments, who should pay, what should be the size of the compensation, and what should be its form. All of these issues will be subject to intense dispute, so that outcomes are difficult to predict. Conflicts over distribution will be intensified, if there are important heterogeneities among the bargaining groups and if information problems restrict the bases for negotiation over shares. In the absence of compensating side payments, some parties may see themselves made worse off by the proposed change, while others will benefit. Distributional conflicts and efforts to address them can block institutional change or so mold the rights arrangement that ultimately emerges that it bears little resemblance to that which was initially proposed.

Time and precedent play important roles in determining the range of feasible contracting outcomes. As a legacy of past informal or formal agreements on property rights, some parties will have a vested interest in the status quo and can be expected to oppose institutional change unless they can be made better off. However, it may not be possible to achieve such an improvement and still maintain the character of the proposed change. Groups with vested interests may have advantages in political bargaining relative to other groups through lower costs of collective action. Their current position in the system binds them together to make them a relatively cohesive bargaining group. They also will have beneficial ties to established political processes and leaders. These advantages will make vested interests effective political lobbyists, biasing institutional change toward maintenance of the status quo.

Legal precedent also will have an impact on how property rights are changed in response to new economic conditions. Precedents set expectations among the various parties for successful institutional change. If the political and economic systems are reasonably open to new entrants and there is a history of routine adjustments in property rights, then institutional change to meet specific economic problems is more likely. In this case, as pressures from new market conditions mount, interest groups will mobilize to lobby for adjustments in property rights, drawing upon the history of past changes. On the other hand, in less open societies where the status quo has been maintained by influential parties, new external market conditions will not bring the same expectations for institutional change. Depending on the size of the market pressures, the lack of expectations for change will limit the expected returns from forming interest groups within established political structures to lobby for new property rights structures.

The roles of time and precedent suggest that there may be an historical path dependence for institutional change. How constraining past decisions are for shaping the subsequent range of feasible property rights and economic activities over time in a society is an empirical question. It is unclear whether generalizable predictions regarding these effects can be made. It seems clear, though, that past property rights decisions will serve to limit the menu of possible institutional solutions to varying economic problems.

THE IMPLICATIONS OF HISTORY FOR SUCCESSFUL INSTITUTIONAL CHANGE

Recent historical investigation also suggests that a less optimistic view of property rights change is in order. This conclusion is based on examination of the role of interest groups and conflicts among them over the distributional effects of property law and government regulation. Hurst (1960, 1964), Scheiber (1973), Hughes (1977), and Friedman (1985) view the early nineteenth-century American legal environment as one that largely promoted economic development by supporting an expanded market and by providing an infrastructure for investment, production, and exchange. Inherited doctrines that seemed to clash with the needs of a growing economy were cast aside by courts and legislatures.

In the late nineteenth century, however, for uncertain reasons, the law became less promotional. Instead of a focus on aggregate economic expansion, the law became more directed to the concerns of particular interest groups and their share of national income. Vested interests and distributional conflicts assumed greater importance. According to Friedman (1985, pp. 339, 340): "These interest groups jockeyed for position and power in society. They molded, dominated, shaped American law. . . . These laws cemented (or tried to cement) the economic position of the people that lobbied for them in the first place: the organized trade group." In an effort to better understand the preoccupation with distributional concerns in the late nineteenth century, Scheiber (1981, p. 108) called for detailed studies of legal change to identify the winners and losers "when the law was used to allocate advantages and liabilities." Additionally, Hughes (1977) commented that the political maneuvering over economic gains makes sense as history, law, and sociology, even though it makes no sense as economics, narrowly defined.

Olson's (1982) examination of the varied success of western economies in the post–World War II period also emphasizes the importance of distributional conflicts among interest groups in shaping the institutional structure in ways that determine the pace and level of aggregate economic performance. He argues that those economies that performed less well–the United States, Great Britain, Canada, and Australia–were constrained by powerful interest groups who successfully obtained controls over work rules, production practices, the adoption of new technology, and entry into new markets. Unions and trade associations, according to Olson, relied upon monopoly power and trade restrictions for income and political power and had little incentive to support adoption of institutions that would provide greater flexibility in the economy. Established interest groups with the costs of organizing behind them formed powerful cohesive lobbyists relative to newly emerging groups who might support changes in the status quo. Only the catastrophic effects of World War II in Germany, Japan, Italy, and France on the structure of interest groups allowed for those economies to reorganize and to be relatively more responsive in the adoption of new technology and improved production methods.

FOUR AMERICAN EMPIRICAL CASES REGARDING PROPERTY RIGHTS

The four empirical cases of property rights change examined in this volume illustrate the contracting complexities described above. They reveal very different levels of success in mitigating the losses of the common pool, despite large aggregate gains from agreement. Moreover, each has a rich, but different history of private and political contracting behind the observed property rights arrangement. This diversity is surprising, because all of the property rights examined involve ownership of natural resources in the United States, which ostensibly offers a very positive environment for private property rights. The cases cover a variety of contractual outcomes regarding the assignment of property rights, ranging from relatively uncontroversial and unabridged private mineral rights, assigned in the mid-nineteenth century; to more limited, attenuated property rights to federal range and timber lands, assigned in the late nineteenth century; and to chronic common pool fisheries and crude oil reservoirs, where under the rule of capture, private property rights are assigned to fish and to oil only upon extraction. Typically, in these two cases, property rights are not assigned to the resource stock, but instead are granted only as a right to extract.

There is a progression across the cases in the complexity of contracting the degree to which clearly defined exclusive rights were assigned to individuals. For example, agreements on private mineral rights were made quickly with periodic adjustments in the law to reduce ownership uncertainty and to correspondingly promote investment and production. Subsequent allocation of federal agricultural land in the nineteenth century was much more controversial, and the conflicts among competing claimants helped to mold the land policies that were adopted. The assignment of private property rights was delayed and in some cases blocked. In the cases of fisheries and crude oil extraction, property rights agreements have been limited both by the nature of the resources and by conflicts among claimants over the distribution of the gains achieved by mitigating common pool losses. For both fisheries and crude oil, costly regulatory arrangements have been instituted, but many margins have remained for dissipation of resource rents. The focus of analysis in this volume for these four cases varies. For the first two cases, which address efforts by various claimants to devise property rights to land and to obtain federal government recognition of those claims, attention is directed to political maneuvering among competing private claimants, politicians, and bureaucrats in shaping federal legislation. The goal is to explain why private property rights to federal mineral lands were established rapidly and endorsed unabridged by the federal government, while private property rights to federal range and timber land were much more difficult to establish politically. For the remaining two cases, involving regulation of fishing and crude oil extraction, the focus is directed more to the problems encountered in negotiations among fishermen and oil producers to devise rules for reducing rent dissipation. In the latter cases, the contracting history is very rich so that an analysis of the bargaining stands of the competing parties is possible.

In Chapter 2 an analytical framework is presented to examine contracting for property rights. The framework isolates the determinants of the aggregate benefits and costs of institutional change, the contracting parties involved, and the factors underlying the calculation of individual private net gains. In this way, the framework provides a basis for determining whether or not parties have incentive to support adjustment in property rights at any point in time to mitigate common pool losses and the political conditions under which contracting is likely to be successful. It shows that efforts to resolve disputes over the allocation of the gains from new property rights arrangements will not only prolong contracting, but mold the agreements that can be reached, with important implications for economic behavior.

2

Analytical framework

INTRODUCTION

The nature in which property rights are defined and enforced fundamentally impacts the performance of an economy for at least two reasons. First, by assigning ownership to valuable assets and designating who bears the rewards and costs of resource-use decisions, property rights institutions structure incentives for economic behavior within the society. Second, by allocating decision-making authority, the prevailing property rights arrangement determines who are the actors in the economic system.

Because of these very basic and critical roles in influencing economic activity and the distribution of wealth and because of the wide variety of property rights arrangements that exist, it is important to analyze how various property institutions emerge. Although these issues have been introduced in Chapter 1, to go further a framework for analyzing the development and modification of property rights institutions is necessary. In this chapter, a conceptual framework is outlined to analyze four different property rights solutions to common pool problems encountered in exploiting natural resources in the United States. While addressing these four cases, the approach taken here can be generalized for examining other property rights issues.

The analytical framework is a very microoriented one. It focuses on the political bargaining or contracting underlying the establishment or change of property institutions, and it examines the motives and political power of the various parties involved. This approach is taken because ownership structures are politically determined, and they assign both wealth and political power in a society. Property rights are viewed here as being more than remnants of past legal and social traditions, although they are affected by them, and as being molded by political maneuvering and bargaining among many competing interest groups. The stands taken by influential parties and the concessions made to reach political agreement on the allocation and definition of rights critically fashion the institutions that are adopted at any time. Accordingly, it is important to identify the parties involved, the determinates of their bargaining positions and political power, and the factors that can lead either to the establishment of new or modification of existing property rights institutions.

The process of defining or changing property rights is referred to broadly in this volume as *contracting,* and contracting includes both private bargaining to assign or adjust informal ownership arrangements and lobby efforts among private claimants, politicians, and bureaucrats to define, administer, and modify more formal property institutions. Because the underlying forces are viewed to be the same, in the analysis of contracting, no distinction is made between creating a property right that never existed and negotiating to change an established right in response to new market or political conditions.

In contracting over proposed property rights, the bargaining stands taken by the various parties depend upon how they view their welfare under the new arrangement relative to the status quo. Estimates of the likely net gains or losses from institutional change faced by each party require an evaluation of the overall productive possibilities with the new property rights arrangement and the distribution of rents it authorizes. The bargaining parties must see their welfare improved or at least made no worse off in order for them to support institutional change, and each party has incentive to seek as large a share of rents under the new arrangement as possible. This competition for the range of economic opportunities made possible by changes in property rights is costly to society. Competition among the contracting parties uses resources, and it leads to changes in the definition and assignment of property rights that affect the nature and size of the aggregate benefits that are possible. The rent-seeking literature outlined by Buchanan, Tollison, and Tullock (1981) emphasizes the importance of these costs. In the case examined in this volume, the competition for resource rents and the political agreements made to resolve disputes over them lead to property rights institutions that would be difficult to explain without an analysis of the political contracting underlying them.

Accordingly, the analytical framework focuses on the distributional issues encountered in political negotiations to define property rights and assign wealth. There are numerous grounds for disagreement over rental shares, and those conflicts can severely limit or block institutional responses to common pool problems. Perfectly compensating side payments could be used to facilitate agreement, but as described below there are formidable problems in reaching a political consensus on side payments because the transfers they involve can become an assignment of rights in themselves. As a result, the side payment schemes reached through the political process may be too incomplete to resolve the distributional conflicts needed for more than minimal institutional change to occur at any time. Even where side payments can be devised, they are unlikely to compensate all the relevant parties, leading some to be made worse off relative to the status quo. Although the proposed property rights arrangements may offer important aggregate benefits by resolving common pool problems, they will be opposed by those who expect to increase their share of the resulting social gains. These bargaining issues, along with the more standard problems of defining and enforcing property claims, determine the nature of the property rights agreements that ultimately emerge.

In developing the analytical framework, three questions involving contracting to assign or change property rights are addressed. First, what are the losses of the common pool that motivate individuals to contract for property rights? Second, what factors lead to pressures to change existing property rights institutions? Third, what can go wrong in contracting?

WHAT MOTIVATES CONTRACTING FOR PROPERTY RIGHTS?

Primary motivations for contracting for property rights are common pool losses. Capturing a share of the expected gains from mitigating common pool conditions encourages individuals to establish or to modify property rights to limit access and to control resource use. The classic articles outlining common pool problems are those by Gordon (1954) and Cheung (1970). Their analyses are built around open access fisheries, but the implications of their arguments apply to other settings as well.

Following Gordon, in the extreme open access case, where there are no controls on entry, individuals are attracted to valuable resources, so long as their private marginal costs of access and production are less than or equal to the average returns for all parties from resource use. In these circumstances, resource values and average incomes fall for several reasons.

First, because property rights to the resource are not assigned, individuals in their production decisions do not have to consider the full social costs of their activities. Their production lowers the productivity of others who are using the open access resource so that the net private and social returns from individual production decisions diverge. In these circumstances, total output by all parties exceeds the social wealth maximization point, where social marginal costs equal social marginal returns. By equating only their relevant private marginal benefits and costs, individuals exploit the resource too rapidly at any time, relative to interest rate and price projections. Further, competitive pressures under conditions of poorly defined property rights encourage short-time horizons in production, leading user costs and other long-term investment possibilities to be ignored. The incentive to invest is reduced because investors cannot anticipate that they will capture any of the resulting returns.[1]

Second, resource values fall because exchange and reallocation of the resource to higher-valued uses becomes more costly and less effective if property rights are absent. Demsetz (1967) argues that an assignment of property rights is a prerequisite before decentralized, price-making markets can form to define asset prices, which reflect underlying demand and supply condition and to facilitate socially valuable exchange among economic agents. Without the more complete market signals possible when property rights are well defined, resources may not flow smoothly or routinely to higher-valued uses as economic conditions change. This can be a particular problem in the allocation of resources over time, because one of the important roles of market prices is to reflect the present value of the intertemporal stream of resource rents. Where those values are higher from future, rather than current use, competitive market pressures will lead to delay in the exploitation of the resource. If property rights and associated market prices are absent, there will be little incentive for economic agents to postpone resource use to the future. Hence, where common pool conditions are prevalent, the value of the resource will be reduced and the economy will be less responsive to current and future opportunities. This reduction in resource values can be exacerbated by ownership uncertainty. To maintain claims to valuable assets or to wrest control from others through the use of force, competing claimants have incentive to divert labor and capital inputs from socially valued production to predatory and defensive activities.[2]

These common pool losses define the gains that are possible from contracts by competing parties to assign more exclusive property rights to resources for controlling access and use and for promoting exchange. The benefits of more exclusive property rights have been described by Alchian and Demsetz (1973) and others. Nevertheless, as Coase (1960, p. 39) noted, the existence of common pool losses does not necessarily

[1]The relationship between security of property rights and the incentive to invest in new technology, for example, is examined by Isaac and Reynolds (1986).

[2]For discussion of the use of force in reallocation of claims, see Umbeck (1981).

mean that it is in society's interest to take actions to more completely define property rights: "But the reason why some activities are not the subject of contracts is exactly the same as the reason why some contracts are commonly unsatisfactory – it would cost too much to put the matter right." Whether or not the more complete defining of property rights is socially beneficial depends on the magnitude of common pool losses, the nature of contracting costs to resolve them, and the costs of defining and enforcing property rights.

In three of the four cases examined in this volume the immediate losses of potential common pool conditions appear to have been large, and they outline the gains to the bargaining parties from the establishment of more exclusive property rights. For example as described in Chapter 3, the gold and silver deposits located in the far western United States in the midnineteenth century required a reasonably clear definition of mineral rights to promote exploration, mining, and milling by private parties. The ore deposits were on unsettled federal lands, where there were no established procedures to allocate private mineral rights. Because of the potential value of the land and the absence of existing property rights arrangements, widespread violence and insecure tenure were quite likely as various claimants competed for control of the most valuable lands. Had these conditions materialized, mining production, even for the surface ore that was relatively easy to extract, and investment in the costly tunnels and processing mills needed for accessing valuable deep-vein mineral deposits would have been limited. The economic consequences of the absence of a recognized mineral rights structure were seen clearly by nineteenth-century miners. They organized quickly and successfully to define property rights so that the promised gold and silver bonanzas could be theirs.

In the case of federal timber and range land in the late nineteenth century, examined in Chapter 4, there also were incentives to establish exclusive rights to land. As settlement moved to the Far West, competition for remaining lands increased. The routine assignment of property rights, which characterized earlier private claims to federal lands to the east, however, required amending federal land law to allow for commercial claims to timber land and for larger claims to arid range land beyond the 160 acres normally authorized per claimant. Unfortunately, unlike the mining case, contracting problems, due to a larger number and more heterogeneous group of claimants and related political tensions over the distribution of the land, blocked agreements to revise federal land law. The extent and pace of the assignment of property rights to land were narrowed, and common pool conditions emerged in some areas. Overgrazing of open range lands became an integral part of the history of land use in certain areas.[3] To a more limited extent, some federal timber lands were subjected to rapid harvest or timber theft, and land rents were dissipated as individuals attempted to circumvent the restrictions of the federal land laws.

Chronic common pool conditions have been a characteristic of fisheries, examined in Chapter 5, where increasing fishing pressure in the absence of property rights to fish stocks has led to declining catch per unit of effort and falling incomes. Further, overharvests have so depleted some valuable fish stocks, such as the California sardine fishery, that whole species have been made more vulnerable to damaging fluctuations in weather and ocean conditions.[4] The losses of open access fisheries have long been recognized, yet in many cases, private contracting and government regulation to limit fishing pressure and to increase rents in fisheries have been only marginally successful. Problems encountered include disputes over the allocation of fishing rights, concerns over the distributional impact of new regulations on existing fishermen, and legal restrictions on the assignment of private property rights to fish stocks.

Finally, in the fourth case examined in Chapter 6, common pool losses have plagued crude oil production in the United States since the first commercial discoveries were made in 1859. With common oil reservoirs accessed by multiple, competing firms, each firm has incentive to drill wells and to extract oil as rapidly as possible. This allows them to increase their share of oil field rents by capturing migratory oil and by taking advantage of subsurface pressures that lower extraction costs. In the aggregate, however, these individual firm incentives lead to higher production costs than would occur if property rights were defined to the reservoir. Costs are increased through the drilling of redundant wells, construction of excessive surface storage facilities, and premature use of artificial lifts to remove the oil. As with fisheries, the losses of common oil extraction have led to various private and government efforts to devise ways of controlling crude oil production. Nevertheless, arguments over the distribution of oil reservoir rents have constrained both the property rights institutions and the regulatory efforts that could be adopted.

Capturing a share of the gains from reducing common pool losses provides incentives for competing interests to contract to assign property rights. If a rights arrangement can be agreed to, it may, however, be only

[3]How extensive was overgrazing and the nature of its costs in the late nineteenth and early twentieth centuries is not known. Some of the costs and the history of overgrazing are described in Gates (1968), but he fails to link insecure tenure to overgrazing.

[4]See Higgs (1982) and McEvoy (1986) for discussions of common pool problems in some American fisheries.

a short-term solution. Dynamic forces within the economy may upset existing equilibria and lead to new pressures to revise property rights.

WHAT FACTORS MOTIVATE INDIVIDUALS TO CONTRACT TO CHANGE PROPERTY RIGHTS?

Pressures to change existing property rights can emerge from the following factors:

1. Shifts in relative prices.
2. Changes in production and enforcement technology.
3. Shifts in preferences and other political parameters.

In effect, these factors may serve as shocks to prevailing equilibrium conditions regarding property institutions, where the benefits and costs of existing arrangements to politically influential parties have been in balance. The first two factors are market forces that can increase the returns to new contracting to change property rights. For example, an increase in relative prices or a fall in production costs will raise the stream of rents attainable from ownership and encourage new competition for control. Old enforcement mechanisms may no longer be adequate, leading to rent dissipation as inputs are diverted from production to protect against trespass and theft. Additionally, the associated rise in ownership uncertainty reduces incentives for long-term investment in the resource and other production plans that would maximize the social value of the resource. Capturing a portion of any rents that can be saved by more precisely defining property rights motivates individuals to organize for collective action to adjust property institutions from their current state to respond to the new conditions.

Because property rights are politically determined, contracting for devoting additional resources for the definition and enforcement of property rights to more valuable assets will occur in the political arena. Informal customs or agreements, which required little or no state intervention and were sufficient in the past, now may be inadequate. However, lobbying politicians and other government officials for new or increased government support for existing private property rights will activate other interest groups in the political process. With many competing interests, greater government intervention in the definition and enforcement of property rights will require concessions in the form of some redistribution of resource rents from current owners to other claimants. As noted by Peltzman (1976), politicians, seeking to maximize votes and other forms of political support, will serve as brokers in responding to the demands of competing interest groups. The ways in which politicians react to the demands of property owners and their competitors will importantly affect how property rights institutions are formalized and how wealth is distributed.

Besides shifts in relative prices and enforcing property costs, changes in the technology of defining and enforcing property rights can stimulate contracting for more precise property rights (Anderson and Hill, 1975; Field, 1985). New technology, which lowers the costs of delimiting individual claims, detecting rule violations, arbitrating disputes, and punishing violators, provides for further gains from applying a more specific assignment of property rights to reduce common pool losses.

These are examples of how market forces can change equilibrium conditions and mold institutional arrangements that are out of step with a new economic environment. Shifts in the political influence of competing claimants also can lead to new contracting for property rights. The sources of political power, the organization of interest groups, lobby efforts to mobilize government actions, and the response of politicians are described in a growing literature that includes Buchanan and Tullock (1962), Olson (1965), Peltzman (1976), Stigler (1971), and North (1981). All things equal, those interest groups with greater wealth, size, and homogeneity will have more resources to influence politicians regarding the assignment of property rights, more votes to attract attention to their demands, and more cohesion to be effective lobbyists.[5]

The effects of market forces and the political power of interest groups in adjusting property rights may go hand in hand. An increase in asset values due to changes in relative prices typically will lead to greater competition for control and political pressure on politicians from various claimants for a more favorable definition of property rights. Current owners as vested interests may have a number of advantages that increase their political power relative to other claimants in political lobbying. Their demands may carry greater political force because they are now comparatively wealthier. Further, they are likely to have established ties to politicians, better understand the political process and institutions, and have lower marginal lobby expenses if past organizing costs are sunk.

Accordingly, politicians often will have incentives to maintain status quo distributions, but as noted earlier, they will do so by balancing competing demands, including those from new claimants. This suggests that no group will get all that it demands. Whether or not existing owners are successful in obtaining a more beneficial definition of their

[5]Dropping ceteris paribus assumptions, there are clear size/cohesion trade-offs. As groups become larger, organizational costs rise. In such cases, entrepreneurial politicians play a role in identifying group interests and in generating group political action. Such politicians bear the organization costs because they expect to capture any resulting political returns through votes and support.

rights as resource values change will depend on their relative political strength vis-à-vis new claimants who are attracted by any increase in rents. New political coalitions will form, and the greater size of the groups demanding some reallocation of property rights and wealth may be sufficient to attract a favorable response from vote-maximizing politicians and from bureaucrats who are concerned with maintaining administrative or regulatory mandates and budget appropriations.

The response of politicians to demands for a modification of property rights will be influenced by the size of the relative price change. The larger the price change, the greater will be the pressure for a redistribution of wealth and, correspondingly, the greater will be the demands by current owners for more protection of existing property rights. The outcome of political bargaining over property rights will depend not only on the political power of the contesting interest groups involved, but it also may depend on how the wealth distributions associated with different interest group demands blend with prevailing distributional norms. A demand for an allocation of property that seems to be extreme relative to accepted practices may broaden the political debate by eliciting a response from other interests who have a stake in the current distribution of wealth. The entry of additional parties in political contracting over adjustments in property rights adds to the demands that must be considered and reconciled by politicians.

These arguments suggest that the political contracting to adjust property rights in response to changing economic circumstances is affected by current conditions regarding the wealth, size, and homogeneity of the various competitors and by broader, longer-term environmental factors that reflect the legacy of past political agreements regarding property rights. These environmental factors, which include legal precedents, distributional norms, and individual expectations regarding the use of the political process to assign property rights, influence contracting costs and the range of institutional alternatives available to address changes in relative prices or technology.

In the United States, distributional precedents, norms, and expectations are specified in the Constitution and in the body of common, legislative, and judicial law. Statutory adjustments in property rights arrangements to address new common pool problems, which are consistent with prevailing distributional expectations, will involve lower political costs for politicians responsible for enacting the legislation than will those that appear to violate established precedents. In the latter case, not only is the legislation subject to rejection by the courts, but so many interest groups may be offended that tenure for the politicians responsible is placed at risk.

To illustrate the legacy of legal precedents that are based on past political agreements for institutional change, consider private property rights to fisheries. In the United States, the common law rule of capture has long determined the assignment of property rights to wildlife, including fish. Under the rule of capture, private rights to fish are assigned only upon catch. Moreover, there is a long-standing legal protection of the low-cost access to fisheries by all citizens. These two legal traditions have contributed to a general prohibition of private property rights to most fish stocks. Ruling out private property rights *a priori* limits the options that are available in the United States for addressing common pool losses in fisheries. Although private property rights may not be appropriate solutions in many cases, in others they may be. The absence of private property rights as an institutional alternative focuses political bargaining on devising regulatory institutions to constrain individual fishing effort and catch.[6]

This section has examined some of the factors that can upset existing equilibria regarding property rights institutions and lead to new political contracting to modify or otherwise redefine property rights. The next section examines some of the problems encountered in contracting either to establish new property rights in response to common pool conditions or to change existing ones, following new market or political conditions.

WHY CAN CONTRACTING TO DEFINE PROPERTY RIGHTS BREAK DOWN?

Capturing a portion of the aggregate gains from mitigating common pool losses is a primary motivating force for individuals to bargain to install or to modify property rights arrangements. The bargaining stands taken by the various interest groups depend upon their private expected gains from institutional change. Each party will attempt to mold the resulting agreements in ways that maximize their share of the aggregate returns. As asserted above, this maneuvering affects both the nature of the property rights that ultimately are adopted and the aggregate benefits that can be obtained.

In considering whether or not to support proposed changes in property rights at any time, the bargaining parties implicitly compare their expected income stream under the status quo with that offered by the new arrangement.[7] The benefits of the status quo are determined by the current property rights allocation and any adjustments in future shares achieved by delaying institutional change. Interest groups may choose to delay agreement on a proposed adjustment in property rights, if they

[6]Scott (1988) discusses the absence of private rights in tide water and inshore fisheries within the English common law.

[7]For a more formal discussion of this framework, see Wiggins and Libecap (1985).

anticipate that new information will be forthcoming to bolster their claims for a larger share of rents in the new arrangement or if they expect favorable changes in political conditions to strengthen their bargaining power. For example, motives for delay existed for some of the firms contracting to unitize oil field production, examined in Chapter 6. Conflicts over the valuation of existing oil leases and shares in proposed unit revenues and costs led those firms that anticipated favorable information regarding the value of their leases to be forthcoming from production to postpone unit agreement. They planned to use the forecasted new information on individual lease values to strengthen their bargaining demands for increases in unit shares. Because the aggregate gains from unitization were greater if the whole field or reservoir were involved, the incentives of some lessees to postpone agreement delayed the formation of the field-wide unit for as much as ten years, even though common pool losses continued in the reservoir.

Despite the possible gains in individual rental shares attainable from postponing agreement on property rights changes, the contracting parties must weigh those gains against their expected private losses from the at least temporary continuation of common pool conditions. In the case of negotiations to establish private mineral rights on Nevada's Comstock Lode in the mid-nineteenth century, the short-run losses from the failure to assign property rights were seen to be large by the initial prospectors who discovered the region, the mining companies that subsequently developed it, and the politicians who were responsible for formalizing the original informal private claims. Without secure private mineral rights, expected mining revenues, the most important sources of income in the region, would have been small because of uncertain land ownership and corresponding limits on investment, mine production, and the exchange of private mineral claims. As a result, negotiations to define private mineral rights began as soon as valuable ore was discovered, and agreements on the assignment of mineral rights followed shortly thereafter. There was little incentive for any of the parties to delay agreement on the process of granting mineral rights. Delaying the assignment of private mineral rights would have prolonged confusion over control of the land, which was anticipated to intensify with the arrival of additional competing miners. Given the large envisioned returns from mining and the limited number of initial claimants, each of the contracting parties expected to benefit from an early definition of mineral rights. The political consensus that emerged influenced the behavior of legislators and judges, and it helps to explain why private mineral rights agreements were instituted so rapidly on the Comstock Lode.

In the absence of serious disputes over the aggregate gains or benefits of assigning or modifying property rights, the heart of the contracting process is maneuvering by the various parties to maximize their individual shares of the wealth possible under the new definition of property rights. Generally, the magnitude of the losses associated with common pool conditions will be uncontroversial because they are observable by most parties. With that public information there will be agreement on the need for institutional change regarding the creation or refinement of controls on resource use. Disputes, however, will arise over how the resulting benefits and costs are to be distributed.

The intensity of political conflict over distribution issues and the likelihood of agreement on institutional change at any time will be influenced by a number of factors, including

1. The size of the aggregate expected gains from institutional change.
2,3. The number and heterogeneity of the bargaining parties.
4. Information problems.
5. The skewness or concentration of the current and proposed share distribution.

Each of these factors is considered below.

The size of the aggregate expected gains

The larger the expected aggregate gains, the more likely a politically acceptable share arrangement can be devised by politicians to make enough influential parties better off so that institutional change can proceed. This suggests that institutional change frequently will occur late in the history of the exploitation of a resource after common pool losses have become so large that distributional issues can be settled. Just how these issues are resolved by politicians, however, affects the nature of the rights system adopted and the social gains achieved. The political process determines how property rights will be assigned and their security.

The number of competing interests

Although large aggregate gains can promote institutional change, the number of bargaining parties involved can make it more difficult. The greater the number of competing interest groups with a stake in the new definition of property rights, the more claims that must be addressed by politicians in building a consensus on institutional change. Politicians, seeking to maximize their political support, must act as brokers and craft trade-offs among the demands of the most influential parties. If sufficient political exchanges cannot be devised, the consensus required for changes in property rights at a particular time to address common pool problems will not be achieved.

The number and political power of the various competing interests that lobby politicians in the process of defining and changing property rights are affected in a critical way by time and precedent. Past political agreements regarding the assignment of property rights define the set of actors who have a critical stake in any subsequent changes in property rights. These vested interests can be expected to organize for collective action to mold political institutions to their benefit. Previous political agreements, which are reflected in statutes and judicial rulings regarding the process of assigning or modifying property rights, also affect political negotiations. Past legislation and court actions help to define both existing property rights and the range of possible institutional changes within the current political system. Hence, they establish precedents and expectations for further collective action by interest groups on property rights issues.

The heterogeneity of the contracting parties

Institutional change also will be more limited if the bargaining parties are very heterogeneous. Important differences across the parties in information regarding the resource, as well as in production cost, size, wealth, and political experience, will make the formation of winning political coalitions and a consensus on the proposed assignment or adjustment of property rights more difficult. In many common pool settings where the parties are heterogeneous and where customs have governed resource allocation and use, the installation of more formal property rights may involve risks for some groups. Those parties who have had informal claims or have been unusually productive under the status quo may be made worse off by institutional change unless their claims or productivity are recognized. Their particular concerns must be addressed in order to reach agreement on the assignment of more precise, formal property rights to reduce common pool losses. In negotiations, prior possession or prior production offers one basis for an acceptable allocation of rights because of the possible availability of public information on past claims and production patterns. These criteria also are popular because they explicitly recognize those parties with significant interests in any adjustments in property rights arrangements. Nevertheless, serious distributional conflicts still may arise with the use of prior possession or prior production as the basis for granting more formally recognized and enforced ownership rules.

Prior production as a criterion benefits those parties who have adapted well to status quo conditions. However, disagreements may develop over the size of their claims if there are information problems in documenting past production. One solution to these information problems is an "equal share" or uniform allocation formula, whereby all parties with past production receive an equal property right. A uniform allocation, however, may seriously disadvantage those who have been the most productive under the status quo, because wealth will be distributed to others under the proposed new arrangement. If very productive parties expect the redistribution of wealth to be large relative to their share of the losses of continuing status quo common pool conditions, they will oppose institutional change.

The other related criterion for a formal assignment of rights, prior possession, often is politically attractive, because it reflects the existing distribution of property and wealth. However, the formal acknowledgment of informal prior possession claims can raise distributional objections if it seems to endorse a very skewed or concentrated allocation of property rights, which may be the case if the parties have very heterogeneous holdings. Skewed distributions based on informal prior possession claims may be tolerated because they are viewed as temporary and are not formally recognized by the state. More formal recognition of such claims, however, may be less politically acceptable and trigger the opposition of other claimants, because state endorsement implies more permanence and security for the distribution of rights and wealth.

Side payments are a way of adjusting shares or property rights to mitigate the political opposition of influential groups. The range of feasible political exchanges for building an accord, however, may be quite limited when the parties are heterogeneous. Side payments or political exchanges require agreement among politicians on the identification of who should pay the compensation, who should receive the wealth transfers, and the form payment should take. Cash transfers may be too explicit a payoff to be politically acceptable within the existing political environment, so other forms of exchange or favorable assignment of property rights must be devised. Whether or not politicians will recognize the demands of certain groups for compensation depends upon group political influence and their ability to extract wealth transfers as the price of building a political consensus for the proposed property rights arrangement.

Information problems

Information problems can complicate an accord on the political side payments needed for institutional change, even when politicians agree on the principle that such transfers must be made. Compensating side payments involve a political consensus on the amount to be paid or the nature of share adjustments. This in turn requires agreement on the value of current holdings and of any losses that some parties expect as a result of the new definition of property rights. The valuation of individual wealth under current and proposed property rights can be a serious problem in political negotiations when there are information asymmetries among the parties regarding the value of individual holdings. These disputes will occur quite aside from any strategic bargaining efforts if private estimates of the value of current property rights and of potential losses from the new system cannot be conveyed easily or credibly to politicians and the other bargaining parties. In that case, political accords on share adjustments or other compensation either may not be reached or achieved only with great difficulty, delaying institutional changes to address common pool problems.

In addition to honest disagreements on the values of individual claims, the information problems encountered in devising side payments will be intensified if the parties engage in deception. Deception can be used to increase the compensation given as part of a political agreement on a new property rights arrangement. It occurs through willful distortions of the information released by various interest groups to inflate the value of current property rights and the losses institutional change might impose. Widespread deception by competing interest groups can make political agreements more difficult by reducing any trust that might otherwise promote the more rapid evaluation and consideration of individual claims in side payment negotiations.

The concentration of the current and proposed distribution of wealth

Two additional factors affecting the costs of political agreement on institutional change to address common pool losses are the relative concentrations of wealth under the current and proposed assignment of property rights. All things being equal, very skewed rights arrangements lead to political pressures for a redistribution of wealth. This can encourage institutional change if wealth is so highly concentrated that relatively few have a stake in the current system. In these circumstances, vote-maximizing politicians can build political support by adjusting property rights both to reduce common pool losses and to reallocate resource rents. Opportunities for economic and social mobility, for accessing capital, and for exchanging property rights within the current arrangement, however, can mitigate political pressures for redistribution. With economic mobility, the wealth assignment over time will be seen as more flexible and more parties can anticipate improvements in well-being.

On the other hand, institutional change to address common pool problems may be blocked or slowed if the proposed distribution within the new rights arrangement is very concentrated. In these circumstances, enough influential parties may see their welfare made worse or at least not improved by the change that political support for it does not materialize. This seems to describe efforts, described in Chapter 5, to revise federal land laws in the late nineteenth century in order to increase the amount of land that could be patented under the land laws by ranchers and lumber companies. The demands of those two groups to increase the size of their claims beyond the 160 acres generally authorized for more profitable development of range and timber land were opposed by homesteaders and conservationists, the principal competing interest groups. These groups argued that their opportunities for claiming federal lands (or, in the case of conservationists, for mandating the "wise" use of land) would be reduced seriously if the demands of ranchers and timber companies were met. The political opposition of homestead interests and conservation groups was made more effective because the changes in the land laws proposed by ranchers and timber companies appeared to violate past distributional practices for federal lands.

A reading of the history of federal land policy (Hibbard, 1924; Peffer, 1951; Gates, 1968) suggests that Congress found the low-cost patenting of small parcels of federal land by millions of claimants and the associated creation of small farms to be politically popular. These land distributions were long-standing, and the changes desired by commercial timber companies and ranchers would have required major adjustments in the law. Because these proposals appeared to concentrate the benefits of federal land on a few and potentially to harm other more influential interests, no significant adjustments in the law were made to promote the patenting of large tracts of land. There were too few possibilities for political exchanges or side agreements between the advocates of changes in the law and those who opposed them to allow for institutional change.

This discussion has highlighted some of the issues that can lead contracting over changes in property rights to break down, even in the presence of significant common pool losses. In a political environment where various interest groups compete to maximize their share of the rents and where politicians must balance those demands in structuring the new arrangement, the reconciliation of conflicting goals may not be achieved to allow for institutional change at any particular time. Subsequent changes in relative prices, costs, and political power, however, may alter the environment so that new bargaining to change the structure of property rights can occur.

To better understand the political negotiations underlying property rights and the interests of the parties involved, the following section discusses the roles of private claimants, politicians, and bureaucrats. Before turning to that discussion, however, a short summary is provided to review some of the other more commonly recognized costs of marking and enforcing property rights that also can influence the nature and timing of the adoption of property rights institutions.

The costs of marking and enforcing property rights are a function of the physical characteristics of the resource, its value, and the political conflicts over the nature of individual shares. The costs of marking, monitoring, and enforcing property rights are greater if the resource is migratory or is generally unobservable. For example, the definition and enforcement of property rights is costly for migratory resources, such as subsurface ore veins. Violations of individual claims to these resources will be difficult to monitor and to police, because ownership boundaries often will be unclear and the amount of the resource held by each owner will be only approximately known. On the other hand, private rights to observable, stationary resources, such as surface ore deposits and grazing or timber land, can be assigned and enforced at relatively lower cost. For these resources, individual claim boundaries can be marked clearly so that trespass and theft can be quickly determined. Similarly, with clear boundaries the range for dispute between rival claimants is narrowed, so that fewer resources will be needed to arbitrate conflicts. These arguments suggest that property rights arrangements to mitigate common pool losses will be more complete for stationary, observable resources, than for migratory, unobservable resources. With these concepts in mind, the next section turns to the contracting parties.

THE CONTRACTING PARTIES

Isolating three general categories of interest groups in order to highlight incentives and bargaining positions will facilitate the analysis of political contracting for establishing or changing property rights. The categories are private claimants, politicians, and bureaucrats; within each group are important differences in incentives that can influence the path of institutional change.

Private claimants

This category includes the broad groups of individuals within a society who claim decision-making authority and rents from asset ownership and use. These groups consist of incumbent owners, who seek the police power of the state to enforce their ownership claims; new claimants, who seek a redistribution of property rights and wealth; and third parties, such as financial institutions and other debt holders, who have a stake in the assignment and security of property rights. Private claimants bargain among themselves for the establishment of informal rights arrangements where the allocation and use of property is governed by custom. More formal definitions of property rights through more explicit state intervention in their assignment and enforcement requires collective action by private claimants in a larger political arena. Competing private interest groups form coalitions to increase their political influence; they lobby politicians for state endorsement of a beneficial assignment of property rights; and they negotiate with bureaucrats to secure favorable administrative rulings. The political influence of private interest groups depends upon their wealth, size, and group homogeneity.

Politicians

Politicians have the authority to direct the coercive power of the state to define and enforce particular property rules. Politicians include both incumbent legislators and judges and those who seek their offices. In competition for political support, both incumbent legislators and office seekers vie for the votes and financial support of influential constituents in determining their stands on property rights legislation. Because not all demands for favorable property rights can be met, trade-offs must be devised by politicians in responding to the competing lobby efforts of various interest groups. The expected political benefits and costs from reacting to each group will determine the nature of the trade-offs or side payments fashioned by legislators and, hence, of the property rights legislation enacted.

The relationship between private claimants and judges in political contracting is less straightforward than it is between private claimants and legislators, because many judges hold life tenure to their office and are less vulnerable to direct political lobbying. Moreover, although lobbying of legislators is accepted practice, political protocol requires more careful and subtle pressures on judges in property rights issues. Nevertheless, because judicial rulings are critical in resolving disputes and in molding property rights, efforts to influence the appointment and opinions of judges can be expected.

Bureaucrats

Groups of bureaucrats have the authority delegated by legislators to implement government policies regarding the definition, enforcement, regulation, and use of property rights. Even though they can act as agents for both politicians and private constituent groups, bureaucrats are more than passive respondents to their interests. Bureaucratic agencies have independent concerns, including maintaining and expanding jurisdictional turf and budgets, that require the cultivation of supportive politicians and private claimants.[8] In negotiations to build political coalitions, bureaucrats can exchange advantageous administrative rulings for the political support of client groups and politicians in congressional oversight and appropriations committee hearings.

Negotiations in the political arena among competing private interests, politicians, and bureaucrats determine how and when the society will respond to common pool pressures by assigning or adjusting property rights. An examination of the political contracting underlying ownership institutions is necessary to understand how property rights are established and modified and why such a diversity of arrangements exists.

IMPLICATIONS FOR THE EMPIRICAL ANALYSIS

The analytical framework described in this chapter outlines the determinants of the aggregate benefits and costs of institutional change, the contracting parties involved, and the sources of conflict over distributional issues. It describes the motives of the various competing interests in political bargaining over property rights. The framework identifies some critical problems that can be encountered in reaching political agreement and how the concessions that must be made in the process influence the property rights system that is adopted. A number of implications can be drawn from this discussion to help guide the empirical analysis described in Chapters 3 to 6.

1. All things being equal, the greater the size of the anticipated aggregate benefits of institutional change (the greater the losses of the common pool), the more likely new property rights will be sought and adopted.

2,3. The larger the number and/or the greater the heterogeneity of the competing interest groups, the more likely distributional conflicts will block or delay institutional change.

4. Distributional conflicts will be intensified if there are known serious information asymmetries among the competing parties regarding the evaluation of individual claims.

5. The greater the concentration of wealth under the proposed property rights allocation, the greater the likelihood of political opposition and the less likely institutional change will be adopted without modification by politicians.

[8]The constraints on discretionary bureaucratic behavior are described with respect to the Federal Trade Commission by Weingast and Moran (1983). An examination of the motives of bureaucrats to expand the size of their agency and the link to bureaucratic salaries in the federal government is in Johnson and Libecap (1989).

3

Contracting for mineral rights

INTRODUCTION

Of the four cases examined in this volume, efforts to assign locally recognized private mineral rights and subsequently to adjust state and federal land law to recognize those contracts were the most routine and uncontroversial. Agreements within the mining camps to outline procedures for claiming and enforcing private mineral rights were completed rapidly, and there appears to have been broad-based political support for incorporation and refinement of the mining camp rules into state and federal law. The history of these efforts is examined in this chapter. The reason for contracting was potential common pool losses, which emerged with the discovery of fabulously rich gold and silver deposits on previously unclaimed and unsettled federal land in the Far West between 1848 and 1890. Private claims to parcels of land were made as miners rushed to the region following the ore discoveries, but there was no existing legal framework for formally recognizing or protecting those mineral "rights."

Competitive pressures for what were effectively, open access mineral lands were intense. For example, within months of the first ore discoveries on Sutter Creek in 1848, the population of California rose from a few thousand to 107,000 and by 1860, to 380,000, with most people concentrated in the mining camps of the central Sierra Nevada foothills. In the absence of legal rules to assign ownership of the valuable mineral lands, there was the potential for violent contention for control. Uncertainty about ownership was a likely result, because none of the competing groups had a monopoly in the use of force to claim and hold mineral land. The historical record suggests that the first miners were concerned that this environment would not support extensive prospecting and mining to access the ore and that the promised bonanza might not be theirs.

In response to these concerns, miners quickly formed over 600 mining camp governments in the Far West to devise local rules for recognizing and enforcing private mineral rights. There was a common pattern for contracting across the mining camps as described by Shinn (1948, pp. 160–2):

> A few hours' labor convinced the discoverers that the royal metal was there in paying quantities . . . soon the news spread; and within a week there were fifteen or twenty men at work in the . . . bed or creek. At first the camp had no organization or government, and every man's conduct conformed to his own ideas of right and justice. Each miner had chosen a "spot to work in," and no question of encroachment could possibly arise until in the widening circle their operations began to approach each other. About the close of the first week after the establishment of the camp, the near approach of two miners' operations caused a dispute about the size of the claims. One of the miners considered his rights infringed upon; and a few days later, after a good deal of talk, his friends circulated an informal oral request through the camp, whose population had by that time increased to fifty or more, asking for a miners' meeting in the evening.

Through these mining camp meetings the squatters' rights of the miners were recognized and local rules were devised for establishing, exchanging, and protecting private mineral claims.[1] The mining camp regulations were incorporated subsequently in state legislation and judicial rulings throughout the West. Moreover, they were specifically recognized in the federal Mining Laws of 1866 and 1872, which allowed for the private patenting of federal mineral land. Within this legal framework private property rights were assigned, refined, and made secure.

THE CONTRACTING ENVIRONMENT

Incentives to contract and the reasons for rapid agreement

Using the implications outlined at the end of Chapter 2, a number of reasons can be identified as to why mineral rights agreements were completed rapidly and were refined repeatedly to avoid some of the losses of an open access or common pool resource. First, the expected aggregate gains from the establishment of private property rights were large, and most of the contracting parties expected to share in those gains. In these circumstances, concessions could be made in bargaining within the mining camps and among politicians within the state legislatures to reach agreement without disruptive distributional conflicts.

The possible losses from the absence of any recognized ownership of the mineral lands provided the incentives for miners to agree on mineral

[1]For analysis of mining camp rules, see Hallagan (1978), Libecap (1978a, 1978b, 1979), and Umbeck (1977a, 1977b).

rights arrangements. The gold and silver discoveries were made on federal lands in advance of general settlement, without any provisions in federal land law for the establishment of private mineral rights. The thousands of miners who were attracted to the ore deposits had no formal institutions for staking claims, receiving title, or arbitrating disputes. Given the value of the land, violent competition and uncertain control were recognized as likely outcomes.

The need for secure mineral rights to promote investment and the realization of the potential of both surface and, later, deep-vein mines was emphasized repeatedly as the mining region was settled. For example, the San Francisco *Alta California,* January 24, 1861, commented on the growing uncertainty over the control of mineral lands along the Comstock Lode in Nevada (Washoe): "Without some such step (a territorial government or annexation to California) it is becoming apparent that Washoe, with all its mineral resources, will fail to command the confidence of capitalists and thus, come short of that permanent and rapid progress that would otherwise be her lot."

These problems of insecure tenure became more critical as surface ore, which could be accessed with little capital, was depleted and mining turned to more capital-intensive activities. Deep-vein mining, which became common in most parts of the West, required tunnels to be sunk with elaborate structural supports; roads to be built to haul ore, overburden, and supplies; mills to be constructed to separate the ore from its surrounding elements; and extensive aqueducts to be developed to bring water to the mines. Once rights were made secure, equity was exchanged especially through use of the new San Francisco Stock Exchange, to raise capital for the development of the mines.

Besides having so much at stake, a second reason why early miners could reach agreement on mineral rights was because the number of contracting parties typically was small, perhaps 20 to 30 individuals in an early mining camp. Further, the groups were relatively homogeneous with respect to race, culture, skill, and technology so that they had similar experiences and expectations regarding legal institutions and private ownership (Umbeck, 1977b; Hallagan, 1978; Libecap, 1979). Additionally, there generally were no significant, competing vested interests in the mining regions whose claims had to be reconciled with those of the miners. This condition allowed later refinements in the mining camp rules to be made by politicians in the state and federal governments at the urging of the mining industry without serious distributional conflicts.[2] The relative absence of nonmining vested interests

[2]As noted in Chapter 1, the complications provided by competing vested interests in devising flexible institutions is a key point made by Olson (1982) in explaining the relative economic performance of post World War II western economies.

was because gold and silver discoveries were made on previously unclaimed land well in advance of agricultural settlement in areas naturally unsuited for farming. In these circumstances, state legislatures and courts could devote attention to the demands of their major constituents, the mining industry, for the refinement and protection of private mineral rights and the overall promotion of the industry.[3]

Table 3.1 illustrates the importance of the mining industry in the economies of selected far western states in the nineteenth century. Comparative data are available only from 1870, which unfortunately is well after the initial development of the industry and establishment of secure mineral rights through mining camp rules and legislative and judicial actions. Nevertheless, the data reveal that as late as 1870, mining of gold and silver dominated the value of agricultural output, the other major industry, in leading mining states except California. Given the singular early importance of mining and the lack of significant competing lobby groups, western state legislatures and courts could be responsive to the demands of the industry at low political cost. Only in California, where agriculture also developed relatively quickly, did the legislature and courts have to address the competing interests of agriculture when they came into conflict with mining (McCurdy, 1976).

A third reason why mineral rights agreements could be reached was because there were no known critical informational asymmetries among the contracting parties regarding the valuing and marking of individual claims. Initial mining camp agreements were made prior to extensive development, so that information regarding land values was more or less evenly spread among the contracting parties.[4] Ore bodies were stationary, and procedures were adopted in the mining camps for adjusting the size of allowed claims according to expectations regarding their value. Smaller claims based on visible markers, such as trees or rock outcroppings, were allowed in stream beds where placer or surface ore was known to congregate. Larger individual claims were allowed on hillsides where ore locations were more problematical.

For subsurface ore, which was accessed later in development, the potential for disputes among claimants was greater because there was less information regarding the extent and direction of the underground

[3]In this way, the state legislature and courts were promotional in advancing economic growth. For discussion of this phenomena elsewhere in the United States in the midnineteenth century, see Hurst (1964, Scheiber (1969), and Friedman (1985, p. 178).

[4]Libecap and Wiggins (1985), in the context of oil field unitization contracting, found that parties were better able to reach agreement on unit shares if contracts were completed early, prior to field development. In that case, contracting occurred before serious information asymmetries developed among the bargaining parties regarding the value of individual holdings.

Table 3.1 *Relative value[a] of gold and silver production and agricultural production for leading mining states*

	1870		1880		1890	
	Gold and silver	Agricultural production	Gold and silver	Agricultural production	Gold and silver	Agricultural production
California	$25,000	$49,900	$18,600	$59,700	$13,700	$87,000
Colorado	3,700	2,300	20,2000	5,000	28,500	13,100
Montana	9,100	1,700	4,900	2,000	23,700	6,300
Nevada	16,000	1,700	15,700	2,900	8,600	2,700

[a]*Note:* In current thousands of dollars.

Source: U.S. House of Representatives (1874), U.S. Department of the Treasury (1881; 1891), and U.S. Department of the Interior (1894, p. 69).

ore vein. Because of this lack of information and the desire to promote excavation of veins, mining camp rules assigned ownership to portions of the known vein, separating it from ownership of surface land, and procedures were adopted *ex ante* for resolving conflicts and assigning ownership should subsurface veins merge and boundaries become confused. These rights to follow a vein below the surface lands of others were called *extralateral rights*.

The fourth reason for the rapid agreement on mineral rights was that most of the contracting parties expected a share in the aggregate gains from establishing property rights. This expectation appears to have been due to two factors. One was that the valuable ore deposits were believed to be extensive relative to the number of claimants. Second, as examined in the following section, there was a political consensus in the United States that federal land should be distributed quickly and at low cost to individuals on an egalitarian basis (Gates, 1968). Although the federal laws focused on agriculture and did not specifically address mineral rights, in dividing mineral lands and assigning them to individual claimants, miners were following well-established practices in claiming a share of the federal estate. Not only did federal land policy establish a general right to claim land, but it set precedents for a relatively equal distribution of holdings.

The emphasis on an egalitarian distribution is reflected in mining camp restrictions on the size of individual claims and in the requirement that holdings could be maintained only with continued development. There was to be no hoarding or monopoly control of mining districts, at least in early development. Unworked claims were considered abandoned and open for other claimants. Further, the number of claims held by each individual prospector was limited to one, with multiple claims given as a reward only to the discoverer of the local mining district. As rights were formalized and exchanged in a district and as the scale of mining increased, particularly for deep-vein ore deposits, consolidation of private mineral claims occurred. Nevertheless, the staking of new claims in other areas remained subject to the egalitarian restrictions of the mining camp rules.

Perceptions of federal lands and the impact on contracting for mineral rights

As argued above, the lack of divisive conflict over the allocation of private mineral rights was due in part to the frontier environment and optimism which existed in the midnineteenth century. This section examines in more detail the precedents of federal land policies and their influence on the rapid definition of private mineral rights on federal lands.

The miners who rushed to the Far West after 1848 were part of the general transfer of federal lands to private claimants that characterized American economic development in the eighteenth and nineteenth centuries. Until the late nineteenth century, federal land was seen as a source of great opportunity for individual advancement and the overall development of both the American society and its economy. The more or less piecemeal distribution of land to new farmers and the avoidance of large concentrations of ownership seem to have been viewed as critical for forming a cohesive society. The widespread distribution of federal land also offered important political benefits to members of Congress who could use land policy to fashion supportive constituents among groups of voters.[5] The practices used in allocating agricultural land helped to form individual expectations for the later claiming of federal mineral land.

As early as colonial times, access to free or low-cost land was a principal attraction for North American settlement. Although there were early disputes over pricing and the details of distribution, a political consensus gradually emerged that the huge federal estate of over 1,442 million acres was to be open for small farm claiming and settlement (Peffer, 1951, p. 8). The political coalition of actual and potential settlers, canal and railroad builders, and real estate developers and their political advocates in Congress and in federal agencies, such as the

[5]While the political advantages to Congress from the various land policies adopted seem self-evident, much more systematic analysis of federal land policy is needed.

General Land Office, was formidable in molding federal land policies to encourage the rapid transfer of federal lands to private claimants (Gates, 1981).

Following the Ordinance of 1785, which outlined the rectangular system of survey and distribution of land through an arrangement of townships and 640-acre sections, revenues from land sale were given initial emphasis. Land was sold for two dollars an acre, but political pressures quickly mounted for more liberal divestment policies. Various relief acts were passed in Congress between 1806 and 1821 in response to political pressures to benefit those who were encumbered by debt from previous land purchases from the federal government. Moreover, the political gains to vote-maximizing politicians from the speedy transfer of federal land to private claimants led prices to be gradually reduced to $1.25 per acre by 1841. Federal land prices were lowered further by the Graduation Act of 1854, which allowed for progressively lower prices for any land that did not sell at prevailing prices.

The political strength of the call for low-priced land for settlers culminated in the Preemption Act of 1841, which allowed squatters to buy 160 acres of surveyed land *before* it was offered for public auction, and the Homestead Act of 1862, which allowed for patents to 160 acres after meeting settlement and improvement requirements. The acreage restrictions reflected what had been considered adequate for farming in acreas of high rainfall and were designed to ensure that federal land would be open for private entry and settlement by large numbers of claimants.

The federal government only was to be a transitional owner and a referee to ensure that the lands went to *bona fide* settlers and not to *land monopolists*.[6] A nation of small farm owners was thought to provide the distributive balance to be politically conservative and free of the damaging conflicts that characterized Europe. This egalitarian distributional emphasis appears to reflect a safety valve notion that may have influenced congressional policy.[7] Federal land, allocated in small plots and at low cost, could help to mitigate any of the social pressures which were being observed in Europe that might build up in eastern U.S. cities. Immigrants could be channeled to the frontier and reduce the supply of urban workers, thereby maintaining acceptable wages in manufacturing. Although the practical effect of this process has been questioned, it may

[6]In his discussion of equity and opportunity in molding U.S. land disposal policies, Friedman (1985, pp. 230–45) emphasizes a desire of lawmakers to avoid the land monopolies and dynasties that existed in England. Land distribution was aimed at fostering economic growth and creating a large, prosperous, middle class.

[7]For a discussion of the role of ideology in forming political decisions, see North (1981).

have contributed to the political foundation for federal land policies through the midnineteenth century.[8]

Federal lands also were used in other ways to promote the political goals of various politicians. Frontier land was granted to developers in exchange for private internal investments in roads and turnpikes, canals, and railroads. Land grants were made to the states to help underwrite private and secondary education and to establish land grant colleges (Morrill Act of 1862). Federal lands were used to compensate veterans of the Revolutionary War, the War of 1812, the Mexican War, and the Civil War. Finally, additional grants of land were given to homesteaders to encourage the planting of trees on the prairies (the Timber Culture Act of 1873) and to promote settlements in the deserts (the Desert Land Act of 1877).[9]

The enormous extent of federal lands in the midnineteenth century and the optimism they helped to foster for projected individual and general economic advancement served to offset distributional concerns and conflicts. These conditions provided a political basis for the rapid assignment of private mineral rights on remote western lands.

Federal policy with regard to private mineral rights

Miners established locally accepted rules for assigning private mineral rights, but until, 1866, there were no provisions for the federal government to recognize those rules. The policy of the federal government since 1785 had been to retain title to its mineral lands in order to extract rents from them. Congress required that the new states created in the West accept its ownership of mineral lands, and such lands were expressly not included in the General Preemption Act of 1841 and other laws designed to transfer agricultural land. Instead, Congress experimented with leasing mineral lands when copper and lead deposits were discovered in the Midwest. High enforcement costs, however, led to the abandonment of leasing and to the sale of land with lead and copper deposits in 1846 and 1847. Prior to the California gold discoveries beginning in 1848, there was no information to suggest that federal mineral lands were very extensive.

The reservation of ownership of mineral land by the federal government, however, was put to test with the California discoveries. As thousands of miners hurried to the region and staked private claims to the land, the new U.S. military governor at Monterey unsuccessfully attempted to evict them. Many of his soldiers deserted for the mines, and given the remoteness of ore strikes relative to the rest of the country,

[8]For discussions of the safety valve thesis, see Danhof (1941) and Shannon (1945).
[9]A detailed outline of U.S. land policy is found in Hibbard (1924).

there was little the federal government could do at the time to maintain its claims. Under these conditions, miners were left to assign private squatters' rights within the mining camps in a manner similar to the division of federal agricultural lands through claims clubs and other arrangements (Gates, 1968). These mining camp rules became the basis for the subsequent development of both private placer (surface) and deep-vein mining. With the importance of mining in the economies of western territories and states and the political demand for security of tenure, legislatures and courts gave rapid legal support to the mining camp rules by incorporating them into statutes and judicial rulings. Although the statehood acts admitting California and Nevada to the Union in 1850 and 1864, respectively, reaffirmed federal ownership of the mineral lands, there was no interference by Congress with local mining arrangements.

After 1864, however, the position of Congress changed as it considered various bills to seize and to sell the western mineral lands as a means of raising funds to reduce the large Civil War debt. Various tax measures on bullion also were contemplated. These threats to the established mineral rights structure led to lobby activity by the mining industry and by western legislatures to block federal action. For example, on May 20, 1864, the San Francisco Chamber of Commerce sent a memorial to Congress voicing its "surprise and alarm" at the various proposals to seize or tax the mines (San Francisco *Alta California*, May 20, 1864). Other efforts were mounted to secure federal legislation to recognize mining camp allocations and to authorize private patenting of mineral lands.

In 1866, the first federal mineral rights law authorizing the transfer of title to private claimants was passed in Congress through the sponsorship of Senator William Stewart of Nevada. Section 1 of the law dropped any royalty requirements and opened federal mineral lands to private claiming, subject to local mining camp rules. Sections 2 and 3 specified the procedures by which an individual could obtain title. In this way, the 1866 law ratified the distribution of ownership authorized by local mining camp rules. The provisions of the law were kept intact in the Mining Law of 1872, which remains in effect for patenting private hard rock mineral claims on federal land.

CONTRACTING FOR MINERAL RIGHTS ON THE COMSTOCK LODE

The example of the Comstock Lode of Nevada from 1859 through 1880 illustrates the process by which secure private mineral rights were delimited.[10] The Comstock Lode was one of the country's premier mining regions, producing nearly $400,000,000 in gold and silver. During its peak years in the mid-1870s, the Comstock yielded nearly 50 percent of total output of gold and silver ore in the United States and more than double the output of the entire state of California, the next most productive region. Because of its size, its influence on federal mining law, and the fact that it preceded most other deep-vein mining regions – the most common type of mining in the West – Comstock mineral rights served as a model for those adopted elsewhere.

Prior to the major Comstock discovery in 1859, the region was prospected and surface deposits were mined by approximately 100 miners, who produced about $67,000 annually, under informal, oral agreements regarding the access and use of mineral land. Eliot Lord, who studied the Comstock for the U.S. Geological Survey, reported later that the miners in the region prior to the main discovery were "easy humored" and conflicts were rare (Lord, 1883, p. 35). With the Comstock strike, however, ore production rose to $257,000 in 1859 and over $2 million by 1861, as indicated in Table 3.2. Individual miner returns jumped from $5 to $100 per day, so that economic and social conditions changed dramatically. News of the discovery spread so quickly that by 1861, there were some 20,000 miners working over 3,149 claims in an area of one mile by five miles. Most of the claims were staked either along the observed portion of the Comstock vein or on what appeared to be adjacent parallel ore veins.

The growing concentration of competing claims in a small area along the surface outcropping of the Comstock vein after the January 1859 ore discovery resulted in disagreements among claimants and a recognition that the informal, oral rules under which the land was worked provided insufficient security of tenure. Within five months of the Comstock discovery, the increase in population and competition for the best land led to a miners' meeting at Gold Hill, site of the original discovery. Three months later, a similar mining camp government was established at Virginia City, site of subsequent discoveries. Later, a third mining camp was organized at Devil's Gate, also on the Comstock. The meetings, which were similar to those held earlier in the California gold fields, led to local, written rules regarding the assignment, maintenance, and exchange of private mineral rights. The mining camp rules written in 1859 preceded the major increase in population documented in Table 3.2 as well as the development of extensive deep-vein mining. The number of miners involved in the camp meetings in each of the three locations was, therefore, relatively small, perhaps less than 100. Those who arrived

[10]This discussion of the Comstock follows from Libecap (1978a, 1978b, 1979).

Table 3.2 *Population of the Comstock region and value of output*

Year	Population at end of year	Value of output
1858	100	$ 67,000
1859	1,500	257,000
1860	3,444[a] (15,000 in region)	1,000,000
1861	5,603[a] (20,000 in region)	2,500,000
1862	6,500[a] (20,000 in region)	6,000,000
1863	25,000[a]	12,500,000

[a]*Note:* In organized mining camps.

Source: Compiled from Libecap (1978b, pp. 35–6, 67, 74–6).

subsequently were required to follow the established mining camp rules in order to stake private claims.

Claims were recognized on the basis of priority of possession, but individual holdings were limited to a fixed amount of land, and claims could be maintained only through continued development. Mineral land could not be hoarded. The mining camp rules outlined procedures for marking and recording claims, the work requirements to keep them, exchange provisions, maximum claim size, enforcement arrangements, and procedures for dispute resolution. By following the required procedures for marking and recording claim boundaries and for working the claim, each prospector was granted a locally recognized title. The recording requirement served to announce and to delineate individual holdings, thereby helping to avoid concurrent claims by another party. Recording also established the priority of a claim to reduce conflicts over priority of possession.

Boundary specifications were determined by the type of mining involved. Placer claims for control of shallow minerals were made in terms of surface area, such as 200 square feet. Claims to deep veins were defined in terms of the vein and not surface land. Individuals were granted 200-foot slices along the vein's exposed surface or apex. Below the surface, a miner could follow his section of the vein to wherever it traveled, even below the property of others. With the confused geology of the region this provision subsequently led to conflicts, which required additional information regarding the vein and refinement in the boundaries of individual claims. As described below, much of this activity centered in the territorial and state courts. Despite these information problems and related claim disputes, ownership was assigned to the vein to encourage private investment in exploration and development. Had property rights been reserved to the surface land owner and defined in terms of exterior boundaries, such as tree stumps, stream beds, and hill sides, the main portion of the vein was likely to be missed, because the extent and flow of the vein were not observable from the surface. In these circumstances, a miner could engage in extensive and costly tunneling along the vein only to find that the most valuable portion of it lay outside the surface boundaries of the claim. Hence, extralateral rights were designed to raise the expected returns from investment in deep-vein mining by assigning ownership to those who explored and mined the vein under mining camp rules.[11]

After local ownership rights had been established in Gold Hill, Devil's Gate, and Virginia City and the limited surface ore had been depleted, claim exchanges were made from the initial prospectors to those individuals who had access to capital and management skills. These market exchanges reflected the growth of the scale of production with the shift to deep-vein mining along the Comstock. By 1861, 86 mining companies had formed with aggregate capital of $61.5 million, and stock of most of the companies were traded actively on the San Francisco Stock Exchange (Libecap, 1978b, pp. 55–6).

Continued ore discoveries from deep mining within certain Comstock claims and associated disputes over ownership of the most valuable land upset existing conditions regarding mineral rights and led to an increase in tenure uncertainty. One problem was the need for more information regarding subsurface geology and the direction of veins to determine both claim boundaries and priority of possession. Lacking a permanent recognized judiciary, the mining camps had no institutions that systematically could gather such information and use it in resolving disputes. Another problem was that oral exchanges of mineral property increasingly were recanted or disputed as claim values rose more than had been anticipated by the seller. A third problem was that apparently abandoned claims were reasserted by some miners, following ore dis-

[11]No effort is made here to resolve the question of whether the advantages of encouraging investment through extralateral rights (vein ownership) were offset by the costs of resolving disputes over subsurface claims. Given complex geology and limited information regarding subsurface veins, disputes would have occurred even with the assignment of vein ownership to the surface land owner. Resolving the question of whether extralateral rights led to greater conflicts requires more data than are available at this point. A similar question is whether investment and development would have proceeded in a significantly different manner had rights not been granted to those who claimed the apex of the vein. In the case at hand, miners had to act quickly to assign mineral rights without an established body of U.S. law to assist them. The practice of assigning extralateral rights on the Comstock subsequently spread through out the West.

coveries made by others who had subsequently staked claims and mined the area. These problems led to pressures for more formal and permanent arrangements to define and enforce mineral rights and to arbitrate disputes than were possible under the mining camp rules. Under the mining camp, changes in claiming procedures and settling conflicts over claim boundaries or other ownership disputes required an ad hoc assembly of "miners' courts."

The pressures for institutional change were observed by Eliot Lord for the U.S. Geological Survey.

> During the early existence of the mining camp, while prospectors were chiefly occupied in staking off claims, no serious controversy had arisen, though individual bickerings over location boundaries were of daily occurrence. One claim appeared as good as another to most of these inexperienced silver ledge hunters, and there was no strong incentive to wrangle over rock croppings whose value was problematical; but before the close of the year 1860 work upon the principal claims had reached a point where collision was inevitable, and then the geological character of the district and the distribution of the ore deposits became a problem of absorbing interest. (Lord, 1883, p. 97)

The March 7, 1860, San Francisco *Alta California* commented on the growing problem of tenure security along the Comstock: "There are very few claims of any value not in the utmost confusion of title and mystery of description. If there shall ever be established here a judicial system, there is a beautiful prospect of litigation; if there be no courts, then there is too much reason to fear force and violence."

The lack of a permanent judicial system in the mining camps, the rise in claim disputes with increased ore discoveries and population, the greater requirement for investment in deep mines, and uncertainty as to the political jurisdiction that would govern the mining region appear to have led directly to the establishment of the Nevada Territorial Government. Territorial status was granted by Congress in March 1961, approximately two years after the first large Comstock ore strike. The concerns of the first Nevada Legislature regarding mineral rights and the region's most important industry were expressed in an opening address by J. Van Bokkelen, a representative from Virginia City:

> We are called upon to make laws of a peculiar character, to *protect* and *perpetuate* interests that differ essentially from those of most of the other territories . . . the principal resources of this Territory exist in its marvelously rich mines, which for their proper development and advancement require judicious thought and enactments by which titles to them can be secured and permanency given to that class of property, and by such means we may invite foreign (Californian) capital to seek investment among us. . . . therefore, let us so legislate that all

persons abroad having capital to invest may be assured that when they turn their attention here, their rights will be well protected by the laws. (*Journal of the Council of the First Legislative Assembly,* 1862, p. 8 emphasis added)

The changes in the value of the mineral lands and the increased competition for them represent the shocks to equilibrium institutional conditions that can lead to new contracting for property rights described in Chapter 2. The legislative and judicial actions taken by the Nevada Territorial Government regarding private mineral rights after 1861, in reaction to fluid conditions on the Comstock are examined below. The territorial government, itself, was replaced in this process of institutional change three years later in 1864 with the establishment of the Nevada State Government. Two factors appear to have been important in the movement from a territorial to a state government. One was that the territorial judicial system was extremely small with only three judges, who were appointed in Washington D.C. The judicial system was quickly overwhelmed by the number of cases of disputed claims to be considered. Also as described below, the mining companies were dissatisfied with the appointment of judges by the president and preferred to have them locally elected, whereby they might be more sympathetic to the concerns of particular local parties.

The critical nature of the situation under the territorial courts was stressed by Charles DeLong, a delegate to the Second State Constitutional Convention:

Of our 3 (territorial) judges at *Nisi Prius* at this time, one is sick and the others have absented themselves, and thus have blocked the wheels of justice; so that in reality we have no courts at all; although I know every lawyer knows that we have interests in litigation so vast in importance that the parties interested in them could almost afford to pay the expenses of a state government for one year if by that means they could have their rights judicially determined. (Marsh, 1866, pp. 13–14)

Another problem facing the mine owners under the territorial government was the lack of voting representatives for Nevada in the Congress at a time when federal policy was in a state of flux regarding the status of private mineral claims on federal land. The federal government was considering various options regarding the disposal or reservation of its mineral lands and did not formally recognize existing private holdings until 1866. Statehood would provide Nevada with two senators and at least one member of the House of Representatives. Congress approved statehood for Nevada in 1864, and the Comstock mine owners or their representatives were active in drafting the state constitution, which was explicit in its support of mining. The final document was accepted overwhelmingly throughout the territory on September 7, 1864, with Storey County (the Comstock Lode) voting 5,448 for and 142 against the Constitution.

Analysis of legislative and judicial activity by the Nevada Territorial and State governments from 1861 through 1885 indicates that the statutes and court rulings were preoccupied with various problems regarding tenure and control of valuable mineral lands. Between 1861 and 1866 when most of the legislative activity occurred, 47 mineral rights laws were passed in six sessions of the territorial and state legislatures. They addressed various aspects of the conveyance of mining property to reduce the potential for disputes, increased the enforcement of assessments on stock owners to pay for mine improvements, established additional legal institutions to protect claims and to arbitrate disputes, and further outlined the nature of extralateral rights to underground veins (Libecap, 1978a, pp. 349–50). Some examples of the legislation and how they seem to have increased security for mining claims are provided below.

In 1861 An Act to Regulate Proceedings in Civil Cases in the Courts of Justice was passed as one of the first acts of the territorial legislature. The statute detailed how the new judicial system could be used to defend property rights from trespass by describing enforcement and arbitration procedures through the courts. The process of filing complaints, issuing summons and injunctions, and obtaining judgment through trial was outlined. A specific tie to mining property was made in Section 561. This section of the law reaffirmed the mining camp rules as the basis for mineral ownership and placed the enforcement power of the government behind the mining camp allocation of mineral land: "In all actions respecting mining claims, proof shall be admitted of the customs, usages or regulations established and in force in the Mining District embracing such claims; and such customs, usages, or regulations when not in conflict with the laws of this territory, shall govern the decision of the action in regard to all questions of location, possession, and abandonment. (*Laws of the Territory of Nevada,* 1862, pp. 314–435)

The territorial legislature also passed an act Defining the Time of Commencing Civil Actions in 1861 (*Laws of the Territory of Nevada,* 1862, pp. 26–31). Section 4 of this law contained a statute of limitations that prohibited action for the recovery of mining claims unless the plaintiff possessed the claim within two years of commencing action. In part, this was to prevent individuals from dredging up old, dormant claims near rich mines and using them to contest vein ownership. Such actions were termed *vampire suits* because they bled rich mines. Because subsurface claim boundaries were generally still hazy in 1861 given the complex geology of the region, as soon as a mine proved rich, unproductive claims adjacent to it were used as a basis to claim a share of the rents. The prime beneficiaries, then, of the statute of limitations were the established, valuable mines. The statute appears to have been aimed to reduce the number of possible competitors for their wealth. It also seems to have attempted to raise the cost of maintaining claims for blackmail purposes since the owners of such claims would have to continue to work the areas according to local rules in order to remain within the time limit. Passed in 1862 An Act for Protection of Mines and Mining Property (*Laws of the Territory of Nevada,* 1863, pp. 33–4) allowed mine owners to sue neighboring mines for damages from excavations and to prevent trespassing, and it clearly specified how a mine owner could obtain government assistance in maintaining the integrity of his claim. The statute reflected the growing congestion on the Comstock as output rose in 1862 and mine values increased. Under the statute, the plaintiff was to file an affidavit showing the location of the offending parties and stating that they were either trespassing or working their mine in such a way as to damage the plaintiff's property. The district judge was then to follow with a notice to the respondent requiring a response to the injunction proposal. On the basis of the original complaint and the response, the judge was to decide whether an injunction to halt the action of the respondent was in order. If he so decided and issued the injunction, then the judge was required to direct surveyors to examine the situation and report to the court. Judgments against the defendant were to include court costs, damages, and fines, and they were placed as a lien upon his property.

An Act for Conveyances, first passed in 1861 (*Laws of the Territory of Nevada,* 1862, pp. 11–21) and then amended in subsequent sessions of the territory and state legislature, outlawed oral agreements in the exchange of mineral claims. Oral agreements regarding the exchange of mine property were the source of considerable confusion because they could not be substantiated, lacking a written record and, often, witnesses. The act required written and recorded contracts with witnesses as proof of exchange. The legislative committee reporting on the law stated that "compliance with the provisions of this act will more completely settle title to the claim in the purchaser. Such compliance will more effectively prevent litigation concerning such property."[12]

By and large, legislation regarding various aspects of mineral rights was enacted routinely with little controversy. Distributional conflicts did arise, however, over two issues: taxes and foreign ownership of the mines. Politicians (legislators and judges) in the territorial and state governments supported the development of the mining industry in

[12]See Libecap (1978b, pp. 60–6) for a discussion of territorial legislation and its impact on mineral rights.

Nevada through the protection of private mineral rights, but they passed the costs of government support of the industry to general taxpayers. The first territorial legislature exempted mining property from taxation, and subsequent Nevada legislatures through 1867 gave mine owners preferential tax rates on mine incomes. The mine owners lobbied the legislature to maintain that policy.

For example, during 1862, nonmine property was assessed at $1.30 per $100 valuation, while mine gross income, rather than property value, was assessed at a rate of $.30 per $100. Even so, the mining companies resisted paying the low territorial income tax. In 1863, the territorial auditor reported that the Ophir and the Gould and Curry mines had gross proceeds of $8 million, but had paid no taxes (*Report of the Auditor of the Territory of Nevada,* 1864). When the auditor sued for tax payments, the objections of the mine companies generally were upheld by the District Court, but never by the territorial Supreme Court. The difference in behavior by the two courts may be explained by the election of the judges. The district judges were elected in Storey County (site of the Comstock Lode) and were, therefore, more sensitive to pressure from local interests than were Supreme Court judges, who were elected territorywide. Efforts to change the preferential tax treatment of the mines were defeated with intense lobbying of the legislature by mine owners. The proposed 1863 Nevada state constitution, which required equal tax rates for all property, was soundly rejected by a vote of 2,157 to 8,851. Nearly half of the negative votes came from Storey County and the Comstock Lode. A revised constitution without the tax provision was accepted by a vote of 5,448 to 142 in Storey County and by 10,375 to 1,284 statewide (Libecap, 1978a, p. 359).

A second devisive issue was foreign ownership. In 1862 local resentment against absentee ownership (mostly by Californians) of the best lands on the Comstock led to a statute restricting out-of-state corporations. The mine owners, however, successfully appealed to Congress to nullify the territorial law; "Having invited and encouraged the citizens of California to undertake development of the mines in their Territory, they have waited until the moment of fruition to attempt to seize the prize which we have rendered valuable (Libecap, 1978b, pp. 68–70). Beyond these two episodes, however, legislation to protect and to promote private mineral rights had broad political support in the Nevada legislature. Mining was by far the major industry; the principal mines employed most of the labor force; and from 1859 through the 1870s the remarkable production from the Comstock led to economic growth and a sense of prosperity in the region among the general population.

The record of judicial activity in Nevada indicates that the courts also were drawn into conflicts over valuable mineral rights. Over time, court rulings established precedents regarding the characteristics and specifications of claims that would be considered in resolving disputes and introduced new information regarding vein boundaries to help resolve ownership conflicts. Most judicial actions involved arbitrating mineral rights controversies and clarifying claim titles, particularly with regard to underground claim boundaries. With limited information regarding geology and the direction and size of ore veins, there were conflicts over the nature of subsurface claims. The mining camp rules granted ownership on the Comstock to 200-feet strips along the surface exposure of a vein and then to the subsurface portion of the vein between the surface boundary lines. With parallel ore veins, mining claims would be separate and adjacent to one another, but if the veins actually merged, then by mining camp rules, ownership was assigned to the priority claimant. Resolving the competing claims of parallel or merging veins required considerable excavation and development of the mines to reveal information about underground geology.

On the surface of the Comstock Lode there appeared to be several parallel veins, but as tunneling progressed, the veins seemed to merge into a single vein. Most of the early court activity involved resolving whether veins were truly distant. Controversy particularly centered on the most valuable claims on the Comstock, because those were the mines where most of the adjacent and contesting claims were staked. Between 1861 and 1866, the leading mines spent at least $4.5 million on litigation, or 11 percent of total mine production costs during the period. The leading mines were aggressive in using the court system to protect their claims, acting as plaintiffs in 70 percent of all District Court cases through 1866, and most of those were actions of ejectment (Libecap, 1978a, p. 346).

Some of the court rulings resulted from considerable lobby pressure on the judges by the contesting parties. For example, between 1862 and 1864 a series of court cases involved two adjacent mines, the Chollar and the Potosi. Both companies had made separate claims based on the parallel vein theory, but as their independent mining proceeded, the separate veins appeared to merge. The Chollar owners successfully appealed to the District Court to eject the Potosi miners from their vein, and the Nevada Supreme Court upheld the ruling. Shortly thereafter, however, the District Court judge resigned amid allegations that he was paid $25,000 by the owners of the Potosi mine to do so. The new district judge reversed the opinion, and the Potosi company again proceeded to mine its claim. The Chollar appealed the decision to the Supreme Court, but this time, lost. The Chollar owners charged that the Supreme Court judges had been bribed to change their position. A rally of miners was orchestrated in Virginia City against the Supreme Court ruling because it undermined the "single ledge" theory and placed the claims of many of the leading mines on the Comstock in jeopardy. A petition signed by 3,500 miners was presented, demanding the removal of the judges. Noting the pressures, the three Supreme Court judges resigned on August 22, 1864, leaving Nevada without a Supreme Court until statehood was enacted later in the year (Libecap, 1978b, pp. 80–4).

Table 3.3 summarizes both production and court activity for the forty mines on the Comstock Lode. It is clear from the table that judicial activity centered around the most valuable mines, and that the owners of those mines generally were plaintiffs.[13] From 1863 through 1868 the Nevada Supreme Court had thirty-two mineral rights cases with judicial rulings focusing on conflicts between adjacent mining companies over subsurface boundaries and the issue of claim abandonment.

After 1866, however, mining had proceeded to such an extent that information regarding the location and nature of subsurface veins was readily available for use by the courts in mediating disputes among rivals. The support of established claiming procedures and land holdings through statutes and court rulings appears to have made rights so secure that fewer actions were demanded, even though new discoveries on the Comstock continued with output peaking at $38.048 million in 1876. The Nevada Legislature stopped meeting annually after 1866, and the number of new mineral rights laws enacted declined, with only thirty-five additional mining laws passed between 1868 and 1880. Judicial activity regarding mining claims also decreased. From 1869 through 1880 there were only sixteen additional mineral rights rulings by the Nevada Supreme Court. This pattern is shown in Table 3.4, which describes the value of mine output and the number of mineral rights laws and Supreme Court rulings in Nevada from 1858 to 1895.[14]

The record of institutional change with regard to mineral rights described in this chapter is one of a rapid response to potential open access or common pool conditions. Contracting among private claimants to assign the initial rights occurred quickly and smoothly at the mining camp level. Additions to and refinements of those rules were made more or less routinely within the territorial and state governments through lobbying of legislators and judges by mining companies.

[13]Libecap (1979) regresses the number of court suits by mine against variables likely to influence conflict over ownership, including value of output, profits, claim size, and number of owners. Of these, claim size, value of output, and number of owners are statistically significant following standard criteria.

[14]Libecap (1978a) calculates indexes of refinement of mineral rights to estimate annual increases in the precision of rights due to statutes and court verdicts, respectively. He finds that increased specificity in the definition and enforcement of private mineral rights occurred largely from 1859 to 1866.

Table 3.3 *Judicial activity by Comstock mines*

Mine	Value of output (1859–65)	Number of suits where the mine was the plaintiff (1861–6)	Number of suits where the mine was the defendant (1861–6)
Utah	$0		
Allen	0		
Sacramento	220,000		
Sierra Nevada	0	8	5
Union	0		
Ophir	4,900,000	28	9
Mexican	1,500,000		
Central	500,000		
California	100,000		
Kenney	0		
White and Murphy	0		
Sides	0		
Best and Belcher	0		
Gould and Curry	12,200,000	20	7
Savage	4,200,000	22	7
Hale and Norcross	50,000	2	7
Chollar	1,400,000	7	10
Potosi	1,500,000	7	8
Bullion	0	11	4
Exchequer	0		
Alpha	100,000		
Imperial	2,100,000		
Empire	1,600,000		
Bacon	1,500,000		
Eclipse	1,500,000		
Sparrow and Trench	1,500,000		
Plato	1,500,000		
Bowers	1,500,000		
Piute	1,500,000		
Consolidated	1,500,000		
Rice	1,500,000		
Confidence	500,000		
Challenge	100,000		
Yellow Jacket	3,900,000	24	8
Crown Point	400,000	12	3
Kentuck	0		
Belcher	1,500,000	9	4
Segregated Belcher	0		
Overman	100,000	18	5
Caledonia	0		

Source: Calculated from Libecap (1979, Table 1, pp. 378–9).

Table 3.4 *Value of Comstock output and legislative and judicial actions regarding mineral rights in Nevada*

Year	Output	Number of mineral rights laws passed	Number of supreme court rulings
1858	$ 67,000	0	NA[a]
1859	257,000	6	NA
1860	1,000,000	0	NA
1861	2,500,000	11	NA
1862	6,000,000	5	NA
1863	12,500,000	6	2
1864	16,000,000	13	8
1865	16,000,000	6	5
1866	11,739,000	6	6
1867	13,737,000	0	6
1868	9,442,000	4	5
1869	6,684,000	0	2
1870	11,382,000	3	1
1871	10,645,000	0	1
1872	12,631,000	3	2
1873	22,390,000	0	0
1874	22,525,000	8	1
1875	26,023,000	0	1
1876	38,048,000	5	2
1877	37,062,000	0	0
1878	20,437,000	7	2
1879	7,560,000	0	1
1880	4,332,000	5	3
1881	1,414,000	0	2
1882	1,675,000	8	0
1883	1,995,000	0	1
1884	2,621,000	6	0
1885	2,952,000	0	1
1886	3,430,000	4	0
1887	3,820,000	0	0
1888	5,665,000	5	0
1889	5,526,000	0	0
1890	4,062,000	4	0
1891	2,733,000	0	0
1892	1,963,000	3	0
1893	1,872,000	0	0
1894	1,281,000	5	1
1895	915,000	0	0

[a]*Note:* NA, not available.

Source: Calculated from Libecap (1978a, Tables 1, 2, pp. 349–54).

SUMMARY

The reasons for the relatively smooth process of institutional change to define and protect private mineral rights include a large expected aggregate gain from the development of the mining industry through secure property rights; broad access to mineral lands under mining camp rules and positive expected individual shares in the aggregate gains of institutional change; few serious information asymmetries regarding the valuing and assignment of individual holdings; a limited number of relatively homogeneous bargaining parties when mining camp rules were established; and the lack of competing, nonmining vested interests in local governments and in Congress. Under these conditions, distributional conflicts did not interfere with the rapid assignment of private mineral rights, and a legal framework was established to mediate disputes and to promote a security of title. The legislative and judicial activities in Nevada clearly had distributional effects in maintaining the allocation of land outlined by mining camp rules and in protecting the mines that developed within them. The initial mining camp distributions, however, were consistent with the broader, egalitarian land division provided by other federal land laws. The guarantees afforded private mineral rights appear to have been important in the development of the mining industry and the economic growth of the region. The mineral rights record is used as a benchmark for analyzing the other contracting efforts examined in this volume.

4

Contracting for changes in federal land policies

INTRODUCTION

Mining camp agreements to assign private mineral rights on federal lands in the midnineteenth century were completed quickly and later, incorporated routinely into state and federal laws, particularly into the federal Mining Law of 1872. Similar efforts made toward the end of the nineteenth century to gain formal recognition of local property rights arrangements to federal range land and to modify the law to allow for the sale of federal timber land, however, were much less successful. Indeed, in many cases the federal government opposed the division of the land practiced and advocated by ranchers and timber companies. Their demands never were incorporated formally into federal land law in the manner afforded the private mineral claims made under mining camp rules. This chapter examines the history of efforts to change federal policy regarding range and timber lands to facilitate private claiming. It outlines the reasons those changes were not made and identifies some of the costs of failing to establish procedures for defining clear property rights to land.

The objectives of ranchers and timber companies were to adjust federal land transfer policies to allow for patents or titles to larger private claims of timber and range land than the 160 acres commonly allowed under the land laws and to relax the requirement for agricultural development as a condition for receiving title. The lands in question were timber lands, largely in the Pacific Northwest, and arid range lands west of the 100th meridian, running from North Dakota to Texas. Neither lands were well suited naturally for agricultural use and disposal in 160-acre plots, which was the practice for eastern federal lands allocated under the Preemption Act, the Homestead Act, and similar land laws. Even though forested areas in the Far West were often mountainous and had greater potential for commercial lumbering than for farming, as in the case of mineral lands, there were no provisions in the land laws for the transfer of land from the federal government to timber companies. Under the law, federal lands were reserved for *bona fide* settlers, and hence, timber companies did not qualify for legally patenting the timber stands they sought to claim and harvest.

There were similar restrictions for obtaining title (patenting) range lands under the federal land laws. Because of arid conditions and poor soil, raising livestock rather than growing crops was the most valuable use of the land. However, sparse vegetation and limited water meant that typically thousands, not hundreds, of acres were required for ranches to be economically viable. Nevertheless, under the land laws ranchers, like timber companies, could not legally obtain title to the land they demanded to support their livestock herds.

Initially, the absence of title to the land was not a serious problem, particularly for range land. Prior to 1880, informally made and locally enforced range land claims appear to have been effective property rights arrangements. Ranchers, who settled the high plains before homesteaders arrived in the region, agreed among themselves to assign property rights on the basis of prior possession, and they enforced their land claims through the use of fences and livestock associations, which were similar in purpose to mining camp governments. On federal timber lands, lumber companies relied more on securing title through evasion of the land laws than on informal property rights arrangements. Lumber companies contracted with entrymen to stake agricultural claims under the land laws. Once the entrymen received patents to their claims from the federal government, they transferred title to the sponsoring timber company.

Increased settlement pressures and competition for the land after 1880, however, made the informal rules of ranchers insufficient for delimiting and protecting private claims. Further, with greater enforcement of federal land laws the procedures of timber companies for obtaining patents became more risky and less effective. Like the mining companies before them, timber companies and ranchers sought to modify federal laws to recognize their holdings and to allow for the rapid transfer of title from the federal government. Absent those changes, ranchers were faced with the forfeiture of at least part of their acreage and timber companies were provided with few opportunities to secure federal timber lands. The proposed adjustments in federal land policy were opposed for a number of reasons. One was that although there were potential common pool losses from insecure tenure, they were not large enough in the late nineteenth century to pressure Congress and to provide the basis for political bargains over the shares of the aggregate gains of agreement. Second, the proposed changes advocated by ranchers of timber companies would have modified a long-standing emphasis on the piecemeal allocation of federal land to small farmers. Further, the adjustments in federal land law were presented to Congress when the frontier was ending and the amount of remaining federal land was declining. Recognizing the land claims of ranchers and facilitating patents by timber companies would have precluded continued access by homesteaders, who had long been favored by federal land policy and who had important political support in Congress and in federal agencies. With a smaller land base, greater weight had to be given by Congress to the claims of homesteaders and others than had been necessary in passing the Mining Law of 1872.

THE CONTRACTING ENVIRONMENT

The nature of federal land law and the impact on patenting federal timber lands

Through 1862, large amounts of federal land were transferred to individual private claimants through cash sales and military script, which could be redeemed for land. After 1862, with enactment of the Homestead Act, federal land policy generally was one of piecemeal divestiture in 160-acre plots to promote small farm development. Nonagricultural activities did not fit well with this scheme. However, the major nonagricultural activity, besides mining, was commercial lumbering in the Great Lakes states of Michigan, Wisconsin, and Minnesota, and it relied on early land acquisitions through cash sales and script.[1]

By the time lumbering reached the forests of California and the Pacific Northwest, cash sales had been abolished and script available for land purchases largely had been exhausted. Other than railroad land grants, there were no provisions in the land laws for commercial timber claims. Ownership of 160-acre plots of timber land could be obtained only by *bona fide* settlers for domestic use under the Preemption Act, the Homestead Act, and Timber and Stone Law.

This stricture posed an important problem for the development of commercial lumbering in the rich virgin forests of the Pacific Northwest. By this time, many logging operations were highly fixed-capital intensive, requiring spur railroad lines and other equipment for the transport of logs. There were economies of scale in cruising timber for the best stands and in harvesting. Efficient lumber operations, therefore, required both secure property rights to support the fixed-capital investment and large amounts of timber land for production. Beyond the use of railroad lands, neither were available under existing federal land laws.

[1]For discussion of the assignment of property rights to Great Lakes timber land, see Johnson and Libecap (1980a).

The restrictions on private patents to federal timber lands brought two behavioral responses. One was an incentive to illegally and rapidly harvest federal timber lands. Given the remoteness of the region, federal timber lands were vulnerable to clandestine, rapid cutting. The overall effect in the late nineteenth century, however, was likely to have been small. Most lumber production at the time centered in the Great Lakes states, which had large stands of timber near growing urban markets. Nevertheless, the commissioner of the General Land Office annually charged that trespassers were denuding federal timber lands in the West and selling the timber to buyers in South America, China, and Japan. As early as 1868, the commissioner predicted that unless the forests were protected in some way, the lands west of the Mississippi would be deforested in 40 years (U.S. Department of the Interior, 1868, p. 187). In 1874 and 1875, the commissioner labeled federal timber lands as "a common property which is preyed upon" (U.S. Department of the Interior, 1975, p. 18).

Regardless of the accuracy of the commissioner's charges, they contributed to the political climate regarding the disposal of federal lands. In the midnineteenth century the popular solution to any depredation of federal land appears to have been the more timely and complete assignment of private property rights. For example, in 1874 General Land Office Commissioner Burdett called for the cash sale of all timber lands to expedite the transfer of land to private parties.

> I am strongly of the opinion that the wisest policy the Government can pursue in respect to this class of lands is that which will most speedily divest it of title in the same for a fair consideration, for the reason that depredations of an enormous extent are occurring, which existing laws are powerless to punish. (U.S. Department of the Interior, 1874, p. 7)

A Public Lands Commission was established by Congress for the first time in 1879 to investigate problems with the disposal and use of heterogeneous lands in the West. The commission included the commissioner of the General Land Office, James Williamson; head of the Geological Survey, Clarence King; and three nongovernment members, Alexander Britton, Thomas Donaldson, and John Powell. The commission gathered testimony regarding range and timber lands at various locations in the West. A common plea was for more lenient federal laws to reflect variations in land quality and production potential and to provide for the speedy patenting of private land claims. For example, John Wasson, U.S. surveyor-general in Tucson, Arizona, stated: "Provide an honest, ready way to procure timber land by purchase, and you will, in my judgement, most thoroughly protect unsold timber, insure *(sic)* the best economy in its use in general, and most certainly encourage its reproduction" (U.S. House of Representatives, 1880, p. 1).

In response to testimony such as this, the Public Lands Commission called for the classification and sale of the varied western lands according to their best use (U.S. House of Representatives, 1880, p. ix, xix–xxii). For instance, the commission argued that "the timber lands should be sold, and a law should be passed to this effect. Will not private ownership, self-interest, best protect this class of lands?" (Donaldson, 1184, pp. 541–2). While the suggested revisions in the land laws were debated in Congress, they were not enacted as the political climate began to change, leading instead to tightened requirements for patenting and to the reservation of some lands by the federal government.

A second consequence of restrictions on private patenting of federal timber lands was the resort to fraud to circumvent the restrictions in the land laws. The use of fraud may have resulted in the greatest rent dissipation for timber lands. Fraud was a more costly and time-consuming means of obtaining title then direct purchase would have been under more permissive land laws. These otherwise "unnecessary" expenses represent a dissipation of some of the rents from owning federal timber lands. The principal way lumber companies could obtain title to federal timber land was through the fraudulent use of the Preemption, Homestead, and Timber and Stone acts. Following federal policy, all three statutes allowed agricultural settlers to claim up to 160 acres of land, but the Preemption and Homestead acts required agricultural use and improvement of the land, whereas the Timber and Stone Act did not. For Homestead and Preemption claims, provisional ownership could be granted by local officials of the General Land Office after six months' residency under the commute provision of the Homestead Act, and after one month under the Preemption Act. Title was sent from Washington, D.C. after the applications were processed. Both laws required proof of improvement and payment of $1.25 per acre. Under the Timber and Stone Act, however, claimants merely had to pay $2.50 per acre for an ownership certificate from the local land office. Of these three laws, the Preemption and Timber and Stone acts especially were used to acquire federal timber land in California, Oregon, and Washington.

Under the three laws the applicant was required to swear that he "did not apply to purchase the same on speculation, but in good faith to appropriate it to his own exclusive use and benefit; and that he has not directly or indirectly, made any agreement or contract, with any person or persons whomsoever, by which title he might acquire from the Government . . . should inure" to others (Copp, 1883).

Fraudulent use of the land laws to acquire timber lands is discussed in the *Reports of the Commissioner of the General Land Office,* particularly the reports of 1885, 1886, and 1887, in congressional hearings on the California Redwood Company case, and in a volume by a former timber company agent, S. A. D. Puter (Puter, 1908). These accounts provide background on how the restrictions of federal land law were avoided through fraud.[2]

Timber companies contracted with agents in the Pacific Northwest to locate and secure desirable timber land. The agents hired cruisers to select attractive timber stands and entrymen to stake claims under federal law to the relevant plots of land. Entrymen often were brought in from other parts of the country or hired from the crews of ships. At the land office each entryman presented himself as a legitimate agricultural claimant. As soon as the certificates of ownership were received from the land office, they were passed to the agent, who then sold them to the timber company. For land claims made under the Preemption or Homestead laws, the entrymen also had to build makeshift cabins and, in some cases, actually occupy the land as required by the land laws. Because the Timber and Stone Act did not have development requirements, entrymen were used merely to file for the property.

Circumventing federal restrictions on ownership of timber land increased the transactions costs of obtaining the land beyond the stated government price and, hence, likely delayed the application for title. The uncertainty of ownership obtained through fraud also may have increased harvest beyond optimal rates, because the General Land Office did attempt to enforce federal laws, particularly after 1880. Greater enforcement of the land laws raises the possibility that fraudulent claims would be discovered and the timber lands desired by the company lost. In those circumstances, the company would have incentive to harvest as quickly as possible. In the case of Preemption claims, entrymen were required to offer proof of settlement and improvement of the land, and periodic field checks were made by land office officials to ensure compliance with the law. Data exist for estimating the size of the added transactions costs or rent dissipation involved through the use of fraud to acquire federal timber lands.

Empirical evidence regarding the dissipation of timber land rents are presented in Tables 4.1 and 4.2. Table 4.1 lists fifteen land fraud cases from 1875 to 1903 with entrymen payments and the price per acre paid by the timber company to the agent upon the transfer of title. The data indicate that the price was approximately six dollars to seven dollars per acre and did not vary significantly whether the Homestead Act, Preemption Act, or Timber and Stone Act was used nor did the price change much from 1875 to 1903. Such a finding is consistent with the sequential

[2]For discussion of the use of fraud to acquire federal timber land, see Libecap and Johnson (1979).

Table 4.1 *Fraudulent timber land claims*

Year	State	Entrymen payments	Price received by agent from final purchaser (per Acre)
1875	California	NA[a]	$5–$7.5
1882–3	California	$50	NA
1882–3	California	NA	$4–$5
1883	California	$150–$200	NA
1883	California	$50	$7
1883	California	$150	$7
1884	Washington	$50–$125	NA
1890	Oregon	$515	NA
1890	Oregon	$320	NA
1898	Oregon	NA	$4
1900	Oregon	$150	$5.25
1900	Oregon	$100	$5.50
1901	Oregon	NA	$5.25
1901	Oregon	NA	$5.65
1902	Oregon	$150	$6
1903	Washington	NA	Up to $11

[a]*Note:* NA, not available.

Source: Calculated from Libecap and Johnson (1979, p. 136).

nature in which land was claimed, moving from the most accessible to more remote, less desirable plots.

Expenditures on fraudulent land claims are more clearly shown in Table 4.2, which details expenditures made by the California Redwood Company in acquiring land under the Timber and Stone and Preemption laws in 1883. The company employed approximately 400 entrymen in its attempt to acquire 57,000 acres of redwood. Payments were made to entrymen, timber cruisers (hired to locate the best timber stands), and agents as well as for other expenses. Agent commissions are the residual after the expenses have been deducted from the total sale revenue of $1,120 for each 160-acre claim. The procedure used for these calculations corresponds to the actual practice. Once the agent and the timber company had agreed on a price, the agent bore the costs of actually locating the claiming the land. His returns depended on the sale price to the timber company and the costs of claiming.

These data in Table 4.2 are used to estimate the size of the timber land rent dissipation that resulted due to the inability of timber companies to directly patent the land under the land laws. In calculating this

Table 4.2 *The costs of the use of fraud to claim timber land*

	160–acre claims	
	Timber and stone $2.50 per acre	Preemption $1.25 per acre
Land cost under each law	$ 400	$ 200
Entryman payments[a]	50	150
Timber cruiser payments	25	25
Cabin and development expenses[a]	–	50
Bribes to Land Office officials	25	25
Miscellaneous expenses[a]	25	25
Agent earnings[a]	595	645
Total (equals sale price to final purchaser at $7 per acre)	1,120	$1,120
Evasion costs (dissipation of rents)	$ 670	$ 870

[a]*Note:* Items included in calculating the dissipation of rents.

Source: See Libecap and Johnson (1979, p. 139).

rent dissipation, the comparison made is between the observed costs of obtaining title to federal timber land and the hypothetical alternative of unrestricted land sales, where entrymen were unneeded and the costly activities of constructing cabins and fences to be in compliance with federal laws were unnecessary. The rent dissipation figure, therefore, includes only those expenditures attributable to federal restrictions and that involved real resources: agent and entrymen payments, development costs, and miscellaneous expenditures. The resulting figures in Table 4.2 indicate that the added transactions costs of obtaining legal title to the land may have been substantial. For the relatively simple Timber and Stone claims the losses were $670 per 160-acre claim, or 60 percent of the final sale price to the timber company. For Preemption claims where there were added development costs, rent dissipation was $870, or 78 percent of the final sale price. To the extent that the price of $7 per acre (or $1,120 per 160-acre plot) reflects the discounted rental value of the land to the timber company, then the rent dissipation was not a trivial amount.

With these data it is possible to provide an approximate figure for the size of the aggregate rent dissipation due to the use of fraud to claim timber lands in the Pacific Northwest. The focus of this exercise is on six land offices whose districts were primarily timber: Eureka and Redding in California, Roseburg and Portland in Oregon, and Vancouver and Olympia in Washington. Those districts contained much of the region's prime forest land. Estimates of the percentage of fraudulent entries were obtained from *Reports of the Commissioner of the General Land Office.*

In 1885, officials from various districts estimated on the basis of spot checks and field investigations of fraud that from one-half to three-quarters of all Timber and Stone entries and one-half to nine-tenths of the Preemption and Homestead claims were fraudulent. On this basis, perhaps as many as half of the claims made for timber land in these land office districts were illegal. With this assumption, as well as estimates of dissipation per each 160-acre entry from Table 4.2 and data on the number of entries from 1881 to 1907 for the six land offices, it is possible to estimate the costs of evading the law in the Northwest. If as many as 4 million acres were claimed through the use of fraud on the basis of the above assumption, the rent dissipation may have been as high as $17 million, or 60 percent of the sale price of the land at seven dollars per acre over the period 1881 to 1907. This figure is greater than the total receipts obtained by the federal government for the land if it received $2.50 per acre under the Timber and Stone Act.[3] In comparison to the roundabout way in which lumber companies had to acquire land from the federal government, Frederick Weyerhaeuser was able to purchase directly over 900,000 acres of timber land in the Pacific Northwest from the Northern Pacific Railroad (Hidy, Hill, and Nevins, 1963).

These estimates of rent dissipation indicate some of the social costs of the use of fraud. Because of the higher transaction costs, the transfer price of the land for a timber company was approximately $6 to $7 per acre, rather than the $1.25 or $2.50 required under the land laws for agricultural claims. Hence, timber companies would contract with agents to claim land only when its expected value had risen to at least $6 per acre. This higher price, though, would delay contracting between agents and timber companies and the corresponding application for patents under the land laws. Accordingly, the land would have been left longer under open access conditions. Steer's (1938, Table 22) data on western Washington stumpage prices for 1890 through 1907 reveal an average annual growth rate of 14 percent. If timber land values rose at the same rate, then the added transactions costs may have delayed the assignment of private property rights by as much as six years, a factor that would have encouraged additional theft and rapid harvest of timber lands.

These admittedly rough estimates of the dissipation of timber land rents through the use of fraud to obtain title suggest that there were social gains from the revision in the federal land laws as advocated by the 1879 Public Lands Commission. In political debates over reforming the land laws, however, the resource costs of fraud were not raised. Rather, fraud was attacked for its effects on the distribution of federal land. Critics charged that through fraud, large timber companies acquired land

[3]See Libecap and Johnson (1979, p. 138) for discussion of the calculation of rent dissipation estimates.

that should have gone to homesteaders. Moreover, it was feared by some that the large timber companies would too rapidly harvest the lands in the Pacific Northwest as they were alleged to have done in the Great Lakes states.[4]

Efforts by lumber companies to have federal timber land classified and sold as separate from the agricultural land available for homesteading were opposed by homesteaders, conservation groups, the Interior Department, and the Department of Agriculture. No political consensus for major revisions in federal land laws could be reached. Given the lack of direct and legal procedures for obtaining private title, much of the timber land in the Pacific Northwest remained within the federal domain. After the enactment of the General Revision Act of 1891, creating the National Forests, federal timber lands gradually were withdrawn from private claiming at the behest of conservation groups and placed in the National Forests under the jurisdiction (after 1906) of the Department of Agriculture.

The nature of federal land law and the impact on claiming federal range land

There were similar problems for the private patenting of federal grazing lands under the 160-acre divestment policy of the federal government. After 1880, the process of settlement reached the more arid regions in the West. The land there was not well suited to the type of agricultural development practiced in the eastern United States, the model for the federal land laws. In the arid lands of the West, where irrigation was necessary for farming or where 25 acres or more were needed to sustain one cow or five sheep for a year, the 160 acres authorized under the land laws were insufficient for a viable farm or ranch. Further, 1,000 acres were commonly required to support enough animals to achieve economies of scale if grazing (U.S. Department of Agriculture, 1936, pp. 208, 417).

Ranchers, who settled the area ahead of homesteaders, claimed as much as they could legally through the land laws, usually 160 to 320 acres in order to include springs and other water sources. In this way they could control much larger acreage in the vicinity of their patented holdings without title. Ranchers also used prior appropriation as a locally recognized means of informally assigning land ownership, and their claims were recognized by local livestock associations. Through contin-

[4]The charges of conservationists regarding rapid harvest and the so-called legend of inexhaustibility that was alleged to have contributed to it are discussed by Johnson and Libecap (1980a).

ual use of an area, a claim could be delimited as noted by a New Mexico rancher in 1917: "A custom has grown up and become thoroughly established among people of this community that where one stockman has developed water on and taken possession of the range by fully stocking the same that he will not be molested by other stockmen in his possession and enjoyment of such range."[5]

Ranchers used various means to enforce their prior appropriation claims. One way was through continued occupancy of the land and heavy grazing, which could lead to more intensive harvest than otherwise might be optimal. Continued stocking and overgrazing of the land reduced its attractiveness to others and made entry less likely.[6] The costs of overgrazing to define and enforce land claims against other potential users were noted by a New Mexico rancher in 1915:

> I can better afford to take the $2,500 loss of stock which I know I will have when the dry years come, than to take my stock off my range and try to save some grass, which I know I will need in those dry years. I hold my range now only by having my stock on it. If I take my stock off, someone else will take my range, and I can afford to lose the stock better than to lose the range. (Wooten, 1915, p. 28)

Ranchers also defined and enforced their prior appropriation claims against other claimants through cooperation with other ranchers through livestock associations. Livestock associations appear to have become common by the mid-1880s, and they had similar purposes to mining camp governments. Typically, the associations had rules regarding entry and use of the land, including restrictions on the number of animals that could be placed in common herds, limits on who could have animals in the herd, the delineation of individual land holdings, registration of private livestock brands, and specification of the labor each rancher was to contribute to the herd (Dennen, 1976). Herds were pooled to capture economies of scale in herding, and association members agreed to control breeding within the herd, to cooperate in the branding of young animals, and to monitor the drift of livestock.

The livestock associations announced the land claims of their members and refused entry by nonmembers. For instance in 1883, Montana ranchers along the Musselshell River claimed some 3,916,800 acres and announced:

[5]Sworn statement by William Jones, rancher, Eddy County, New Mexico, April 10, 1917. Record Group 49, Unlawful Enclosure, Box 799, U.S. National Archives. Quoted in Libecap (1981a, p. 16).

[6]The practice of overgrazing to limit entry on Indian reservations where grazing rights are poorly defined is developed in Johnson and Libecap (1980b).

We the undersigned, stock growers of the above described range, hereby give notice that we consider said range already overstocked; therefore, we positively decline allowing any outside parties or any parties locating herds upon this range the use of our corrals, nor will they be permitted to join us in any round-up on said range from and after this date. (Stockslager, 1888, pp. 5, 6)

Within the boundaries defended by a livestock association, cooperative efforts were made to control the number of animals placed on the range by each member, because individuals had incentive to overgraze at the expense of others. Generally, the allowable number of animals was based on water ownership:

It will be seen that the ownership of the watering places gives tenure to contiguous range. This fact is recognized by Western cattlemen, and the question as to the number of cattle individual owners are permitted to hold, under regulations of the various local associations, is determined by the questions of water frontage. (Taylor, 1886, p. 316)

The cattle of all members grazed together, and annual cooperative roundups were held for branding and marketing. Livestock associations also required each member to supply bulls based on the number of cows in the association herd to ensure the spring's calf crop. Moreover, the timing of breeding was controlled, so that calves were born in the early spring to increase survival chances and to be ready for fall marketing.

Unlike the mining camp organizations, however, the livestock associations in many cases lacked consistent and broad-based political support in the territories and states in which they were located. Because of the size of range land claims and increased competition from homesteaders, the livestock associations became controversial. Violent conflict occasionally broke out as ranchers attempted to protect their range land claims from inroads by newcomers, but their success at controlling entry appears to have deteriorated as settlement advanced (Osgood, 1929, p. 186).[7] With more animals on the range and a decline in the effectiveness of livestock associations in controlling the land as competition increased, ranchers resorted more to fencing their private or club claims. Fencing could more definitely establish control over entry and use of range land, and the rise in land values after 1880 contributed to investment in fences by ranchers on both patented and federal land. The extent of private fencing of federal land is unknown, but available evidence indicates that

[7]Conflicts between livestock associations and new small ranchers and homesteaders make up some of the richest western historical lore. Moreover, disputes among cattle and sheep raisers over grazing territories emphasize the lack of clear property rights and growing tension over control of the land.

between 1883 and 1919 a maximum of 9 million acres may have been illegally fenced in the eleven far western states at any one time.[8]

The General Land Office, which had been organized to process individual land claims under the land laws, became a vociferous opponent of the private fencing of large federal land claims. While the director of the General Land Office had favored authorization of larger claims for arid range land in the 1879 *Public Lands Commission Report,* the position of the agency changed by the mid-1880s. As conflicts between ranchers and homesteaders over the land increased, political pressures on the General Land Office mounted for removal of the "monopoly" control over land held by ranchers. Additionally, as the remaining stock of federal land declined, the agency may have seen that its future lay more in preserving federal land for small claimants.

As settlement extended to the high plains, homesteaders became increasingly frustrated upon finding large tracts of desirable land fenced: "I took up 160 acres of government land. . . . It happened to be in a Big Cattle outfit's meadow and when I went to do my Improvements as required by the laws of the United States of America, this same Cattle outfit shut and locked the gates and forbid me to come on my Homestead. . . ."[9] In 1882 and 1883, General Land Office Commissioner McFarland called for fence removal and the prosecution by the Justice Department of those ranchers who erected them. In 1883, Interior Secretary Teller announced that "this department will impose no objection to the destruction of these fences by persons who desire to make *bona fide* settlement. . . ." (Libecap, 1981a, p. 32). In 1884, both the Senate and the House asked the Interior Department to provide a summary of the extent of illegal enclosures of federal range land that were blocking homestead settlement.

The General Land Office responded with *Unauthorized Fencing of Public Lands* (U.S. Senate, 1884), which argued that vast areas, in some cases whole counties, were fenced. Commissioner McFarland stated:

> I am satisfied from the information received that the practice of illegally enclosing the public lands is extensive throughout the grazing regions, and that many millions of acres are thus enclosed and are now being so enclosed to the exclusion of stock of all others than the fence owners and to the prevention of settlement and the obstruction of public travel and intercourse. (U.S. Senate, 1884, p. 3)

The true extent of illegal fencing of federal lands is unknown, but regardless of the report's accuracy, it helped to fuel the antifencing

[8]See fencing calculations by Libecap (1981a, p. 20).

[9]Letter from Mr. John Thompson, Viola, Wyoming, to the General Land Office Commissioner, November 30, 1921, Record Group 49, Unlawful Enclosures, U.S. National Archives, Box 903. Quoted in Libecap (1981a, p. 32).

pressures in Congress, and legislation was passed in 1885 authorizing the Interior Department to investigate and order the removal of all private enclosures on federal lands. The records of the General Land Office indicate that there was strict enforcement of the 1885 law during the period 1885 to 1887 and then periodic enforcement through 1934. Through 1908, the General Land Office filed suit to remove enclosures that covered over 36 million acres.[10] Even as late as 1902, the agency called for the removal of private fences: "The avowed policy of the government to preserve the public domain for homes for actual settlers has no more implacable and relentless foe than the class that seeks to occupy the public lands for grazing purposes, by maintaining unlawful fences thereon" (U.S. Department of the Interior, 1902, p. 11). The removal of private fences as a control on entry and the increase in settlement through inappropriately small homesteads ensured that competition for use of the open access range would intensify and that harvest pressures would increase.

With secure property rights, the depletion of the stock of range grasses through intensive harvest could have been consistent with wealth maximization as ranchers increased grazing of virgin grass stands to correspond with price and interest rate expectations. However, the grazing pressure that intensified on the *open range* in many parts of the West toward the end of the century appears to have been due more to the common pool nature of the land.[11]

There are no studies of the trend or aggregate impact of overgrazing on the value of range land. From approximately 1900 to 1930, however, experiment stations in the U.S. Department of Agriculture studied particular pastures for the effects of overintensive harvesting. A 1916 Department of Agriculture report described the practices of ranchers who used the open range: "The only protection a stockman has is to keep his range eaten to the ground and the only assurance that he will be able to secure the forage crop any one year is to graze it off before someone else does" (Barnes and Jardine, 1916, p. 16). However, overstocking made herds vulnerable to drought, which further depleted forage stocks, forcing the dumping of animals on the market. For example, in a 1922 study, the Agriculture Department noted: "On an overgrazed range there is never much, if any, reserve feed, so that whenever a drought occurs, the stock must be taken off . . . such forced removals are nearly always undesirable because prices are likely to fall when there is no alternative, but to throw large numbers on the market" (Wooten, 1922, p. 28).

[10]Calculated from figures collected by Libecap (1981a, Table 3-3, p. 20).

[11]Overgrazing receives extensive treatment in the literature on western lands, but the focus is rarely on the problem posed by the inability to define secure property rights to land. For traditional discussions, see Gates (1968) and Peffer (1951).

A 1925 Department of Agriculture experiment station study of 111 ranches in West Texas, Arizona, and New Mexico provides the clearest indication of the impact of tenure conditions on grazing practices and livestock production on range land. In the study, ranches were classified according to their reliance on open access or open range federal land, because climate and topography were similar in the three states. The study included twenty-eight ranches in far west Texas, where 73 percent of ranch acreage was owned by the rancher, with the rest leased and eighty-three ranches in southern New Mexico and Arizona, where only 8 percent of the land grazed was privately owned, with the rest open federal range. Ranch sizes, in terms of cattle raised, in both areas were similar with an average size of 2,305 cattle per ranch in Texas and 2,087 in New Mexico and Arizona. The variables examined in the comparative study were the calf crop, death loss, cow weight, and animal value. The performance of ranches across the three states varied according to tenure conditions. Calving rates were 47 percent higher in West Texas, animal death rates were 54 percent lower, and the average value of cattle was 43 percent higher than in New Mexico and Arizona. The report argued that the differences in animal quality were due to both poorer forage and the lack of incentive for ranchers to invest in improved breeds: "It is futile for an individual to purchase good quality bulls at high prices for use on the open range when inferior bulls of other operators graze on the same range."[12] The higher death losses in New Mexico and Arizona were blamed on poorer forage, which led to starvation or seriously weakened cattle, vulnerable to disease: "There is no doubt that the death losses suffered by ranchmen during the dry years were greater than they would have been if the range had not been stocked according to the amount of feed available in good years."[13]

In assessing federal range land conditions in the early 1930s, the U.S. Department of Agriculture (1936, p. 3) reported that

> There is perhaps no darker chapter nor greater tragedy in the history of land occupancy and use in the United States than the story of the western range. First it was, "The Great American Desert," a vast and trackless waste, a barrier to the gold fields. Unexpectedly and almost overnight it became the potential source of great wealth from livestock raising. And thereon lies the key to the story . . . the major finding of this report . . . at once the most obvious and obscure is range depletion so nearly universal. . . .

This report was likely exaggerated and self-serving for the Agriculture Department, which was involved in jurisdictional conflicts with the

[12]Taken from Parr, Collier, and Klemmendson (1928) as reported in Libecap (1981a, pp. 24–8).

[13]Quoted from Parr, et al. (1928) in Libecap (1981a, p. 26).

Interior Department over administration of federal range land. Nevertheless, the overgrazing due to open access range conditions referenced in the report appears to have been a problem in many areas of the West.

CONTRACTING CONDITIONS AND OPPOSITION TO CHANGES IN FEDERAL LAND LAWS

The implications outlined at the end of Chapter 2 suggest the reasons why efforts to change land laws to facilitate the rapid assignment of private property rights to federal timber and range lands were unsuccessful. One reason was that the aggregate losses of common pool conditions on range and timber lands in the late nineteenth century were not immediate or large enough to offset distributional conflicts and convince politicians of the political gains from changing the land laws. The damage to range lands through overgrazing, where it occurred, was gradual, subject to short-term reversals during periods of unusual rainfall. On those federal range lands where there were fewer competing claims, established ranchers and new homesteaders could proceed with raising livestock and farming without enacting the proposed legal changes. Title to small parcels of land could be obtained under existing legislation, either legally or through fraud. The limited long-run viability of small homesteads on arid lands was not yet understood. Further, the rental losses from the overharvest of far western timber lands also were small because most of the U.S. lumber production in the late nineteenth century remained in the upper Great Lakes states. Railroad lands in the Pacific Northwest also offered alternative sources of timber. The costs of the use of fraud to obtain title to federal timber lands may have been more substantial, but the political debate regarding fraud focused on ethics and the distributional effects of the acquisition of large tracts of land by lumber companies, rather than on the added resource costs of fraud.

A second reason for the failure to reach agreement on changes in the land law was that distributional pressures in the allocation of federal land intensified after 1880 as the amount available for private claiming declined. With less to go around, recognizing the large land demands of ranchers and timber companies would have precluded others from obtaining a share of the federal estate under the land laws. Table 4.3 illustrates some of the factors that helped to shape the political environment regarding federal land laws in the late nineteenth century.

Table 4.3 lists U.S. population, homestead claims and acreage, and the amount of unappropriated federal land for selected years from 1870 through 1930. By 1900, 65 percent of the original federal estate available for claiming of 1,442,627,520 acres had been transferred to private parties or state governments or reserved by the federal government

Table 4.3 *Federal lands and claiming activities*

Year	U.S. population	Homesteading		Remaining Unappropriated Federal land (acres)
		Claims	Acreage	
1870	40,000,000	33,972	3,754,203	708,853,000
1880	50,000,000	47,293	6,054,708	NA[a]
1890	63,000,000	40,244	5,531,678	505,678,000
1900	76,000,000	61,270	8,478,409	498,302,000
1910	92,000,000	98,598	18,329,115	333,075,000
1920	106,000,000	48,532	13,501,100	199,055,000
1930	123,000,000	13,248	4,920,842	177,966,000

[a]*Note:* NA, not available.

Source: Population: U.S. Department of Commerce, Bureau of the Census (1975, pp. A1–8); homesteading and unappropriated lands: Libecap (1981a, pp. 15–16).

(Peffer, 1951, pp. 99–109). Only 498,302,000 acres remained, and much of that was low-value arid range and desert land. The tightening of available federal land led to the announcement in 1890 by the U.S. Census that the frontier was closed: "Up to and including 1880 the country had a frontier of settlement, but at present the unsettled area has been so broken into isolated bodies of settlement that there can hardly be said to be a frontier line. In the discussion of its extent and its westward movement it can not, therefore, any longer have a place in the census reports." (U.S. Department of the Interior, Bureau of the Census, 1892, p. xviii)

The passing of the frontier had serious implications for the continued use of federal land for social mobility (Turner, 1962), and it also occurred at a time of growing concern over possible shortages of many key raw materials (Olson, 1971) and a series of severe macroeconomic recessions. The panic of 1884 was followed by the long depression of 1893 through 1897 and by another panic in 1907. These conditions contributed to a new sense of pessimism and a perceived narrowing of opportunities as noted by Friedman (1985, p. 338): "By 1900 if one can speak about so slippery a thing as dominant public opinion, that opinion saw a narrowing sky, a dead frontier, life as a struggle for position, competition as a zero-sum game, the economy as a prize to be divided, not a ladder stretching out beyond the horizon. By 1900 the theme was 'hold the line'." Further, there was a growing concern about the size of businesses and the potential for monopoly power a concentration of production increased through the organization of pools, trusts, and mergers in key industries, such as railroads, steel, sugar, and meat packing. These concerns contributed to the enactment of the Sherman Antitrust Act in 1890, investigations into alleged monopoly actions in certain industries by the Bureau of Corporations in the Commerce Department and, later, to the establishment of the Federal Trade Commission and passage of other antitrust legislation. This was not a favorable political environment for efforts to change federal land law to allow for the rapid patenting of larger tracts of land by ranchers and timber companies.

A related factor that complicated political negotiations over federal range and timber lands was that there were many more vested interests whose demands had to be reconciled than had existed for mineral lands earlier in the century. The huge initial size of the federal estate, as well as the small-farm emphasis of the land laws, had established expectations for broadly distributed shares of federal land. As millions of acres were claimed, various constituent groups were created including homesteaders, ranchers, miners, timber companies, oil firms, power companies, railroads, land developers, conservationists, politicians, and officials from the General Land Office and the Forest Service and other agencies in the Interior and Agriculture departments.[14] Over the course of the nineteenth century, these groups increasingly competed for the same land and feared that changes in the law to accommodate special problems of one group would deny access to others. This led to a hardening of bargaining positions that had not existed during the earlier efforts to recognize private claims to federal mineral lands.

Homesteaders and ranchers were important antagonists in lobby efforts to shape federal land policies. However, the larger number of voters who were homesteaders, potential homesteaders, and related land developers seems to have made them a more influential political constituency in Congress than were ranchers. Their influence contributed to provisions placed in the Republican and Democratic platforms from 1872 through 1888, calling for federal land to be distributed *only* to actual settlers as envisioned in the Homestead Act. Although ranchers often were politically powerful in local governments, they were small in number relative to other claimants nationwide. Moreover, although they organized into lobby groups, such as the National Cattlemen's Association, to influence Congress, ranchers may not have been a cohesive political force at that time. There were intense conflicts between cattle and sheep raisers and among cattle raisers according to size that may have limited their impact on federal legislation.

A third private constituent group in the political debate over the disposal of federal lands, who opposed liberalization of the land laws, were conservationists. Although small in number, conservationists were

[14]For discussion of the many claimants and issues involved in the distribution of federal lands, see Libecap (1984).

an extremely cohesive group with influential ties to top federal policy-makers. The conservationists opposed further alienation of federal land to *any* private claimant and called for retention of remaining lands. They argued that the government had been too generous in its land policies and that under private property rights and the pressures of market forces the remaining federal lands would suffer. The conservationists argued that socially beneficial use of the lands required continued government ownership and administration of the land through scientific management principles.[15]

The focus of initial conservationist attention was on forest lands under the leadership of Bernard Fernow, Gifford Pinchot, and Franklin Hough, who were influenced by Prussian state forestry efforts. For example, Bernard E. Fernow, chief of the Division of Forestry in the Department of Agriculture in 1886, commented:

> the forest resource is one which, under the active competition of private enterprise is apt to deteriorate . . . that the maintenance of continued supplies as well as of favorable conditions is possible only under the supervision of permanent institutions with whom present profit is not the only motive. It calls preeminently for the state to counteract the destructive tendencies of private exploitation. (Fernow, 1902, p. 20)

Conservationists were critical of what they believed to be excessive harvest rates by lumber companies in the Great Lake states of Michigan, Wisconsin, and Minnesota. They argued that lumber companies harvested too rapidly under the myopic pressures of the market.[16] In political debates over the disposition of federal land, conservationists were critical of the General Land Office and the Interior Department for past land disposal policies.

A fourth constituent with a stake in any changes in federal land policy was the General Land Office. Although the commissioner of the General Land Office had supported the liberalization of the land laws to allow for 2,560-acre homesteads on arid range land, rather than 160-acre plots, in the 1879 *Public Lands Commission Report*, the agency's position changed shortly thereafter. By 1885 and the administration of Commissioner A. J. Sparks, the General Land Office became a strident advocate of homesteading and opposed major relaxation of restrictions on claim size. For example, in 1886 Commissioner Sparks asserted:

[15]The various positions of the conservation movement are outlined in Hays (1959), Barnett and Morse (1963, pp. 17–48, 72–95), and Robbins (1976, pp. 301–98).

[16]For discussion and analysis of Great Lakes timber harvest and the implications of firm behavior, see Johnson and Libecap (1980a).

> I found this great estate of the people rapidly wasting under a system in which the government appeared to have no place except as an agency for its own despoilment. . . . I found illegality and fraud. . . . It has been the object and purpose of all my efforts to maintain the integrity of the laws and to secure the rights of *actual settlers* to actual homes on the public lands. (U.S. Department of the Interior, 1886, p. 3, emphasis added)

Further, the commissioner stressed that

> settlers who go out on the frontier and endure the hardships of pioneer life do so with the expectation that they will be joined by others; that communities will spring up, churches and schools will be established, the value of the possessions enhanced, and the conveniences and advantages of civilized life attained; but speculative appropriations of public lands destroy these hopes and leave actual settlers isolated for years, or they are compelled to remove to other localities. (U.S. Department of the Interior, 1886, p. 45)

Similarly, in 1897 in response to a bill to liberalize procedures for claiming timber lands the General Land Office commissioner argued "there can be no doubt that if this bill becomes a law it will be taken advantage of by persons who want to make money quickly, to acquire the timber lands under its provisions at a very low price and strip the mountain sides of their forest growth as rapidly as possible" (U.S. Department of the Interior, 1897, p. 74).

The position of the General Land Office in the debate over federal lands in the late nineteenth century is understandable. As noted by Libecap (1981b), the agency had been established, funded, and staffed to process private claims under the land laws and was subject to political pressures from homesteaders and from their supporters in Congress. Officials in each local land office also had personal incentives for maintaining the piecemeal distribution of federal land. The registers and receivers in each land office collected fees and commissions from applicants which could be used to supplement their salaries up to a $3,000 limit (U.S. Department of the Interior, 1913, pp. 149–51). Recognizing the range land claims of ranchers would have reduced the number of applicants to be processed and speeded the ultimate disposal of federal land.

With uncertain and, perhaps, relatively small aggregate gains from liberalizing federal land transfer policies, the efforts of ranchers and timber companies failed. With a large number of competing interest groups, demanding shares of federal land, there was no political consensus for major revisions in the land laws to facilitate patenting by timber companies or to recognize the large land holdings of ranchers. Political support could be mustered for only minimal revisions in the federal land laws to better accommodate arid conditions, but these acts were aimed at homesteaders. Under the Kinkaid Act of 1904, 640-acre homesteads were authorized in certain dry areas of Nebraska; in 1909, the Enlarged Homestead Act allowed for 320-acre claims in arid regions; and 640-acre stock raising homesteads were approved under the Homestead Act of 1916. Although these laws promoted new homesteading and were used often by established ranchers to obtain title to additional land, the acreage they authorized for patenting was considerably less than that recommended by the 1879 Public Lands Commission. Thousands of homesteads that were too small for viable ranches or dry-land farms were sold or subsequently abandoned in the early twentieth century.[17] This experience suggests that a more direct method of transferring larger plots of arid land to private claimants from the federal government would have involved lower transactions costs.

Instead of liberalizing the land laws, by the end of the nineteenth century, there was a gradual tightening of criteria for patenting and a reduction in the property rights that could be obtained from the federal government. The General Revision Act was passed by Congress in 1891. The law not only repealed two popular vehicles for patenting federal land, the Preemption and Timber Culture Acts, but it established the national forest reserves. The subsequent permanent reservation by the Federal Government of some 168 million acres of forest land in the lower forty-eight states in the National Forests was a major reversal of the long tradition of federal land divestiture. Further in 1903, a second Public Lands Commission was created to review the condition of federal lands and to recommend policies regarding them to the president and Congress. The commission members included General Land Office Commissioner W. A. Richard, F. H. Newell of the U.S. Geological Survey and the Reclamation Service, and Gifford Pinchot. In its 1904 report, the commission reversed its predecessor's recommendation for 2,560-acre grazing homesteads. The new commission reported that "the general lack of control in the use of public grazing lands has resulted, naturally and inevitably, in overgrazing and the ruin of millions of acres of otherwise valuable grazing territory" (U.S. Senate, 1905, p. xxi). Nevertheless, the 1904 Public Lands Commission supported the continued distribution of land to actual settlers in 160-acre plots. The commission also was critical of those land laws, such as the Timber and Stone Act and Desert Land Law, which were fraudulently used to acquire large tracts of range land (U.S. Senate, 1905, pp. iv–viii, xvi–xviii). Continuing the shift away from the divestiture of federal land, the commission recommended that range land be retained by the federal government. It suggested that grazing

[17]Promises and problems with dry land farming homesteads are described in Hargreaves (1957).

districts be established on range lands to control entry and use and reduce overgrazing (U.S. Senate, 1905, p. xxii). Access to each district was to be granted through grazing leases rather than through the assignment of titles, and limits were to be placed on the number of animals that could be grazed on the land. This recommendation for the establishment of grazing districts and individual grazing leases was not enacted for 30 years until the Taylor Grazing Act was passed in 1934. Jurisdictional battles between the Interior and Agriculture departments over administration of the federal range land explains part of this delay. Eventually, nearly 175 million acres of range land, outside Alaska, was assigned to the Interior Department.

SUMMARY

Unlike the case of private mineral rights where distributional disputes were less serious, federal land laws were not revised to recognize the claims of ranchers and timber companies and to promote the quick transfer of title from the federal government. The use of fraud to acquire timber lands seems to have involved significant costs, dissipating rents on the federal lands involved. Moreover, the evidence that can be assembled suggests that open access conditions on federal range land led to nonoptimal overgrazing in at least certain areas of the West. Nevertheless, distributional conflicts over the disposition of the federal estate could not be resolved in the manner desired by ranchers and timber companies. Ultimately, political negotiations among the competing interests led to the reservation by the federal government of much of the federal timber and range lands. Problems involving the security of tenure, investment, and other land use decisions on those lands continue today.[18]

The problems encountered in attempts to resolve the distributional conflicts associated with the assignment of property rights can be seen in other empirical settings. Chapter 5 shifts the discussion from federal lands to examine contracting problems to resolve rent dissipation in a classic common pool resource, fisheries.

[18]For discussions of the problems with federal lands, see Johnson (1985) and Libecap (1981a).

5

Contracting in fisheries

INTRODUCTION

Although the previous chapters focused on efforts to establish property rights to land and to change in U.S. land policies, this chapter examines some of the contracting issues encountered in attempts to control access and harvests in fisheries, where there often are serious common pool problems. The losses from common pool conditions in fisheries include declining total catch, falling income for fishermen, overcapitalization through too many vessels and too much gear, and excessive labor input. These losses provide important incentives for fishermen to contract among themselves and with politicians and bureaucrats to reduce fishing in order to bring total catch to more optimal levels. Nevertheless for many of the reasons identified in this chapter, the contracting record in numerous fisheries is one of only partial success. Differences among fishermen according to skill, capital, and size create conflicting interests and incentives for regulating fishing. These differences limit the informal agreements that might be reached among fishermen to reduce fishing and diminish the effectiveness of fishermen as cohesive lobbyists for influencing more formal regulatory controls on access and harvest in open access fisheries. As a result for some species, catch and incomes for fishermen have fallen sharply and stocks have been depleted. In response, regulatory policies have been adopted to rebuild the stock and to raise incomes, but they frequently have been very costly and relatively ineffective. In other more extreme cases, overfishing has so depleted stocks of some species that they are no longer commercially viable.

The problems encountered in efforts to reduce common pool losses in fisheries are due to various reasons. One that has attracted considerable attention is the fugitive nature of the resource, which raises the costs of defining and enforcing property rights or other regulatory arrangements. Most species of fish are migratory, some across large areas; accordingly, their location at any time is unlikely to coincide with individual property boundaries or regulatory jurisdictions. Further, in many areas there are multispecies, each with different levels of depletion and stress, requiring distinct programs that often are difficult to manage and enforce separately. Additionally, knowledge of many fisheries is extremely limited regarding the nature and size of the stock, its relationship to the environment, the impact of harvest, and the response of fish stocks to regulatory controls on harvest. These information problems complicate the calculation by individual fishermen of the benefits that might be possible from agreement on new institutional ways of controlling fishing.

The nature of individual benefits or rental shares under the status quo relative to that under a new arrangement is an important aspect of fishery regulation. Understandably, existing fishermen are concerned about how they will fare with changes in regulations and property rights in fisheries. At issue are potential redistribution of catch and income through regulatory controls and other restraints on fishing practices that may be part of the new arrangement. Because of differences in skill and capital, catch and income can vary sharply across fishermen in a fishery. Those fishermen, who have adapted well to the status quo, even to open access conditions, are under risk that their shares of fishery rents with any new program to control fishing will be less than they receive currently. This hazard can exist at least until the fishery is severely depleted. At that point, when individual catch and incomes are very low and many fishermen have left the fishery, those that remain are more likely to see themselves as being made better off with more restrictive controls on harvest, and agreement on new regulatory initiatives is more probable. Unfortunately, by that time society will have absorbed many of the losses of the common pool.

Redistribution concerns not only affect the stands taken by fishermen in bargaining over proposed regulations to limit access and harvest, but also affect the positions of regulatory officials who will be concerned with how the proposals affect their authority and jurisdiction. Politicians, who must enact legislation regarding fishery regulation, are a third group with a stake in the outcome. In devising policies, politicians are interested in maximizing political support, and their efforts to balance the competing demands of various groups will affect the stands they take in enacting legislation. The political influence of fishermen in this process will depend upon their numbers and cohesion as lobbyists. As described below, differences among fishermen, as well as their traditional independence make them an unlikely cohesive political force for enacting restrictions on their own fishing practices. The likelihood of successful collective activity is greater when fishermen are seeking restrictions on their *rivals* or when they are attempting to obtain programs that will raise total catch or wealth without placing tight controls on individual fishing effort.

In political negotiations among fishermen, politicians, and bureaucrats for regulatory policies, those programs that recognize existing share allocations or rankings of fishermen, although increasing total catch or yields, generally will have broad support. If yields can be increased through the adoption of season closures or through the construction of fish hatcheries, existing fishermen can be made better off and no divisive redistribution of catch or fishing effort need be involved. Where restrictions on individual catch or effort are necessary as part of setting a total allowable catch for a species, which may be necessary in more depleted fisheries, incumbent, skilled fishermen will prefer a quota scheme that maintains status quo rankings. Individual quotas assigned on the basis of historical catch will therefore be popular with those fishermen because they recognize past performance and minimize redistribution. On the other hand, new entrants and young fishermen have incentive to oppose any quota schemes that grandfather historical catch patterns or place restrictions on new entry. The regulations adopted will depend in part on the relative political power of the completing fishing groups, and established fishermen may have important advantages in the political process.

The general preferences of fishermen to favor visible, yield-enhancing policies, where costs are spread elsewhere among taxpayers and where more conventional distributional restrictions are avoided, frequently coincide with the interests of politicians and bureaucrats. The latter have an incentive to respond to organized interest group pressures regarding common pool losses in fisheries, while avoiding as much as possible the disruptive distributional conflicts that may be part of more binding restrictions on harvest and access. Accordingly at least in early regulations, politicians, and bureaucrats also will favor those policies that raise total yields and that minimize interference with the activities of more influential groups of fishermen. Such policies, though, may leave many margins for fishery rent dissipation uncontrolled. This community of interests, however, is apt to break down and conflicts among fishermen, politicians, and bureaucrats to increase if conditions in the fishery degenerate further, as is likely, and greater intervention is required. Some of the important sources of contention are addressed in this chapter. The discussion benefits from the work of Anthony Scott (1955, 1979, and 1988).

Another problem confronting fishermen and politicians in the design of institutions to control fishing is the legal prohibition of private property rights in most U.S. fisheries. Although private property rights to the stock granted to individuals or to groups, may not be appropriate in many cases due to high enforcement costs for migratory species or the existence of multispecie fisheries, in other cases they may be a viable institutional response to common pool losses. Their prohibition narrows the range of feasible alternatives for consideration. Both common law as well as legislative and judicial actions, have emphasized the right of all citizens for free access to fisheries and other wildlife (Lund, 1980; Tober, 1981). Federal and state governments historically have refused to assign private property rights to areas large enough to cover widely roving species. Private property rights have been viewed by politicians as interfering with the politically popular guarantees of a right to fish.[1] Moreover, where fishermen have been able to agree on *private group* efforts to control entry and harvest through unions and trade associations, their actions have been opposed by the Justice Department and the Federal Trade Commission as violations of the Sherman Antitrust Act. For these reasons, various government regulatory policies, rather than private property rights or private group controls, have been the principal arrangements for addressing common pool losses in U.S. fisheries.

The experience of the sardine and salmon fisheries dramatically illustrates the common pool problem in fisheries and some of the bargaining issues encountered in addressing it. McEvoy (1986) examines the striking collapse of the California sardine fishery after only thirty years of intensive commercial harvest. The fishery emerged as a leading one in the early twentieth century. With increased demand for food during World War I and for fish meal in the postwar period, harvest of sardines off the California coast rose sharply. Under prevailing open access conditions, the number of fishermen and vessels increased, new harvest technology was adopted, new canneries were opened, and reduction ships were introduced to process sardines into fish meal and other products.

By the late 1930s, sardines were one of the country's most valuable fisheries, with annual harvests exceeding 500,000 tons. During the fishery's peak in 1936–7, 230 seiners delivered 726 tons of sardines to fifty-two processing plants. This level of production, however, was not to continue. By the early 1950s, the stock of sardines was so depleted that it became vulnerable to damaging shifts in ocean temperatures. Annual catch dropped to under 20,000 tons. Despite early warnings of the effects of overfishing, regulatory controls to reduce harvest significantly were not adopted. There were conflicts among the chief regulatory agencies, the California Fish and Game Commission and the U.S. Fish and Wildlife Service, regarding what policies should be implemented, and no sus-

[1]Agnello and Donnelly (1975) describe the granting of private leases to oyster beds. The general discussion of contracting and regulation in fisheries in this chapter draws on that provided in Johnson and Libecap (1982).

tained collective actions among fishermen for private or government controls to help protect the fishery were forthcoming. In the face of new harvest and processing technologies and the use of large reduction ships for converting sardines to fish meal and oil, the pressures on the fishery were too great, and by 1952 for all practical purposes, the commercial sardine fishery was finished.[2]

The case of the Pacific Northwest salmon fishery described by Higgs (1982) is similar, although there were less dramatic effects on the fish stock. For salmon, regulatory arrangements were adopted to limit harvest and to offset the decline in the stock. The kinds of regulations adopted, however, are instructive of the general pressures encountered from various competing interest groups in devising regulations to address common pool losses in fisheries.

Higgs (1982) begins by describing the vibrant nature of the salmon fishery at the turn of the century, when salmon were abundant and could be harvested at low cost due to their anadromous nature. Because salmon returned from the ocean to the streams from which they were spawned to deposit and to fertilize eggs, they could be harvested from fixed sites along streams leading from the Pacific Ocean, using fish wheels and gill nets. A system of private property rights to those sites, similar to the well-developed property systems used earlier by Indians, developed in the region along major rivers, such as the Columbia.

As early as 1892, there were concerns about the entry of new fishermen and the impact on the stock of the growing rise in total gear used in the fishery. Declining productivity created intense hostilities among various groups of fishermen, who were identified by the types of equipment they used. Each group blamed overfishing and its consequences on others and attempted to have the fishing privileges of their rivals curtailed. Gillnetters increasingly were able to secure legislation in Oregon and Washington that placed discriminatory restrictions and taxes on the operators of fish wheels, who operated from fixed sites along streams. Ultimately, the low-cost and very productive fishwheels and the private property associated with them were outlawed by the two states. However, removing one group did not solve the common pool problem in the salmon fishery. Conflicts over access and harvest in the salmon fishery continued among the owners of fish traps in Puget Sound, commercial purse seiners, who relied on vessels, and sports fishermen. New political coalitions of fishermen formed to lobby for restrictions on their competitors. Because of their small numbers and highly visible, large catches, fishermen who used fish traps, as with those who used fish wheels, especially were the subject of redistribution pressures. With the

[2]See also Ahlstrom and Radovich (1970).

growing political influence of numerous sports fishermen and those commercial fishermen who used vessels, regulations eventually were adopted in Washington state to prohibit fish traps.

The new regulations forced the interception of salmon in the ocean at much higher costs. Rather than controlling entry into the fishery with a limited number of fixed sites, under the new arrangements, entry required only a vessel. Capitalization and labor costs increased with time as the number of boats and fishermen rose. As the stock of salmon declined from more intensive harvest, a principal regulatory response was to construct costly hatcheries and to shorten the fishing season in an attempt to raise aggregate catch. The progressive shortening of seasons intensified the rush of fishermen to complete their harvest early and added to pressures for larger and faster vessels. Moreover, tensions among competing fishing groups continued as each sought to obtain legislation that favored it and posed constraints on its rivals. The overall condition of the salmon fishery was ill served by this process.

Higgs (1982, p. 56) sums up the effect of the regulatory policy adopted through this political process as follows:

> the state's solution was to limit the harvest by penalizing or prohibiting the more productive harvesting techniques. In the Washington fishery today fewer than 10,000 commercial fishermen, aided by many millions of dollars worth of fishing gear, harvest about 6 million salmon annually. Before World War I a similar number of men, working with much less than the modern amount of capital, normally harvested three to four times more salmon each year.

Higgs argues than under current costly arrangements the salmon fishery may no longer offer a positive contribution to net national product.[3]

In analyzing the problems encountered in addressing common pool problems in fisheries, the chapter draws on the discussion in Johnson and Libecap (1982). The next section examines the historical emphasis on open access and the legal prohibition of private property rights as a contractual solution to the common pool. The section "The Gains from Contracting and Bargaining Problems" outlines the gains to contracting and the hazards to better fishermen from various regulatory arrangements. Predictions are developed regarding the kinds of regulations that will receive support from fishermen. The section "Emperical Predictions and Evidence" examines the empirical evidence regarding informal contracting to limit common pool losses and the nature of formal regulation of the Texas shrimp fishery.

[3]Regulation of entry and harvest in the Pacific Northwest salmon fishery also has been complicated by the assistance of multiple species, Indian claims, and joint-use agreements with Canada.

THE CONTRACTING ENVIRONMENT: THE POLITICAL EMPHASIS ON OPEN ACCESS

This section outlines some of the legal background in the United States affecting fishery regulation. It offers an explanation for why private property rights to the stock or private *group* regulation of entry and harvest, rather than government controls, have not been widespread solutions to the common pool problem in U.S. fisheries.

Early American wildlife law repudiated the English practice of reserving access to wildlife to those with social distinction. Instead, the law generally emphasized the common property nature of fish and other wildlife, which were to be owned and harvested by all citizens. Fish and wildlife were to be held in trust by the government for the common benefit. This policy followed both from an effort to avoid the discriminatory restrictions that existed in England on individual access and from the sheer abundance of fish and other wildlife in North America, relative to the population in the colonial and early federal periods. This abundance, along with the high costs of assigning and enforcing individual claims to wildlife, which could not be confined easily to private boundaries, lowered the gains from contracting for private property rights and encouraged common property practices. As sources of food and income, fish and wildlife were considered a natural gift, along with the land, that was available for individual use for private gain. Indeed, there appear to be many similarities between federal land policies, which provided for egalitarian, low-cost access to frontier land, and the emphasis on equal access to fish and wildlife. With the free taking of wildlife (as well as land) private ownership was based on the rule of capture, and the resulting distribution of individual harvests and income was left to individual skills and merits.

These common property rules for fish and wildlife initially offered high political benefits with low costs. With vast quantities of fish and wildlife in North America and a small relative population, overharvest was not an issue. Although this was a short-term condition, the political guarantees of nondiscriminatory access had long-term consequences. Constituents with vested interests were created for political guarantees of a "right" to fish by all citizens. Over the course of the nineteenth century, with increased demands, political pressures were mounted to maintain broad access to fish and wildlife. Where private property rights had been established, there were calls that they be dismantled. As a result, by the late nineteenth century, state and federal courts had rejected many of the private fishing sites granted earlier by state legislatures (Lund, 1980).

Government ownership of fisheries for their *common* use by all citizens and the associated rejection of exclusive access restrictions were repeatedly emphasized by federal and state courts in molding regulatory policies. Cases included *McCready v. Virginia,* 94 U.S. 391 (1887), *Toomer v. Witsell,* 334 U.S. 385 (1948), *Stephenson v. Wood,* 34 S.W.2d 246 (1931), and *Dodgen v. Depuglio,* 209 S.W.2d 588 (1948). For example, the Texas Supreme Court in 1950 rejected state legislation to limit entry in Texas coastal waters: "If allowed to stand, the statute and action already taken under it are reasonably calculated to perpetuate, in effect, a monopoly of commercial fishing for the favored class" (*Dobard v. State,* 233 S.W.2d 440). Although lower state courts in South Carolina and Texas sustained legislation that placed discriminatory license fees on out-of-state fishermen, the U.S. Supreme Court and for the Texas legislation, the Texas Supreme Court, reversed those rulings and rejected restrictions on out-of-state residents in devising regulatory schemes as being unconstitutional. Licensing and other limited entry arrangements for inshore and state territorial waters were ordered to include all citizens (*Toomer v. Witsell,* 334 U.S. 385; *Dobard v. State,* 233 S.W.2d 440).

THE GAINS FROM CONTRACTING AND BARGAINING PROBLEMS

Gains from contracting

Following the Gordon model outlined in Chapter 2, where there are no exclusive rights or access restrictions to the fishery, entry by new fishermen and increased capital investment in vessels and equipment will continue at any time until the average cost of catching a standard unit of fish equals the market price. With unlimited entry, the rental value of the fishery can be dissipated through declines in average catch and increases in labor and capital inputs. The disappearance of the commercial California sardine fishery following intensive harvest is an extreme example of the dynamic biological and economic consequences possible with unmitigated open access fishing pressure. Under less severe conditions, the gradual advent of open access or common pool losses are felt by individual fishermen through declining incomes brought on by higher total costs and by declining catches. Avoiding these losses provides incentives for fishermen to contract with one another and with politicians and bureaucrats for collective action to devise regulatory schemes to limit entry and harvest.

Contracting problems

Despite these incentives, there are important differences among competing groups of fishermen that may limit agreement on the kind of regulations to be adopted and the formation of coalitions for lobbying politicians and bureaucrats on how common pool problems should be addressed. Additionally in considering fishery legislation and policies, politicians concerned with maximizing votes and bureaucrats concerned with maintaining or expanding regulatory jurisdictions will have separate agendas that may diverge from the interests of many fishermen. Politicians must balance the demands of various constituents, and their stands on proposed fishery legislation will reflect political compromises so that no group is likely to receive all of its demands. Similarly, bureaucrats have a stake in current and proposed regulatory policies with incentives to support policies that expand or at least maintain their authority over the resource. However, such regulations may not be attractive to most fishermen who are concerned about bureaucratic interference in their fishing practices. The position of various fishermen, politicians, and bureaucrats on fishery policies will depend upon how they view their welfare under the new regulations relative to their position under the status quo.

As noted earlier, all three groups are likely to endorse policies that increase total catch or wealth for fishermen without placing serious constraints on individual catch or effort and without redistributing income. Direct government subsidies and tax relief, hatcheries to build the stock, season closures and gear restrictions to protect adolescent, lower-value fish, and access denials to foreigners through 200-mile coastal zones or to other less influential fishermen, such as the owners of fish traps and fish wheels in the early Pacific Northwest salmon fishery, are examples of policies that are attractive to many incumbent fishermen, politicians, and bureaucrats. Procedures that enhance total catch or wealth in the fishery forestall the implication of more restrictive and controversial controls on the access and catch of individual fishermen. Hatcheries, minimum fish size limits, and fishing seasons to allow juvenile fish to grow can be presented as popular, visible conservation devices, and the costs of these and other programs can be spread across all taxpayers.

Any improvement in conditions in the fishery through the adoption of these policies may buy time and enhance the welfare of existing fishermen. Greater fishing by incumbent fishermen and further entry by new fishermen, however, will be invited, intensifying competitive pressures on incomes and the stock of fish and continuing the losses of the common pool. To arrest any deterioration in conditions and to bring aggregate harvest to more optimal levels, more restrictive limits on individual fishing must be considered. Depending upon how severe is the problem, limits on new entry may be adopted, and some existing fishermen may have to leave. Those that remain will face tighter controls on fishing effort and catch. These policies, though, will be much more controversial and difficult to implement, at least until fishery conditions have so declined that many fishermen already have left and others have incomes that are so low that they see clear benefits from policies controlling access and catch. In the meantime, questions will have to be resolved regarding who (if anyone) should be denied access to the fishery and for those fishermen who continue, regarding the details of how individual catch or effort will be regulated. Because there are important differences in individual catch and returns among the fishermen, the regulatory policies adopted have the potential for placing disproportionate limitations on some groups of fishermen. These naturally will be resisted. Redistributional concerns in political negotiations regarding the policies to be adopted often are heightened by limited information on what the ultimate impact of regulation will be on the fish stock and on the returns to individual fishermen. These information problems make it more difficult for fishermen to determine whether their welfare will be improved by the adoption of new regulations relative to the status quo.

It is useful to explore the heterogeneities among fishermen in more detail to see how they affect the potential for voluntary collective action to address common pool conditions and the stands taken in political negotiations for specific regulatory policies. Although there are differences across fishermen according to type and location of fish caught, size of vessel, and gear used, skill differences are examined here for their effects on contracting. With differences in skill, costs will vary across fishermen for the fixed level of effort. This means that better fishermen will have higher catches and incomes than will their less skilled counterparts under open access conditions. Regulatory policies, however, can redistribute income, depending on how they constrain the access and fishing effort of individual fishermen. Hence, better fishermen can be expected to oppose any arrangement that might place disproportionate restrictions on them and involve significant transfers to others. If adopted, such policies could make more skilled fishermen worse off relative to their position under the status quo. Concerns over the distribution of fishery rents raise the costs of contracting and limit the kinds of agreements to which fishermen can agree. Because of a long-standing egalitarian emphasis in many fishery regulatory policies due to pressures to redistribute income through the political process and because of the costs of designing regulations that respect skill and catch differences, skilled fishermen have reason to be wary of regulatory change.

Differential abilities among fishermen have been recognized in much of the literature on fisheries, although the implications for contracting for fishery regulations generally have not been drawn. Scott (1979, p. 733) notes that "fisheries experts repeatedly speak of durable groupings of skippers, vessels, and crews according to the size of their catch or earnings, year in and year out." Johnson and Libecap (1982) report that Texas shrimpers are categorized by their peers according to fishing skills, which include correctly setting nets and regulating their spread determining effective trawling speeds, and quickly locating shrimp before they are dispersed by the trawling of other fishermen. The effects of variation in skills are observable in persistent catch differences per unit of effort across fishermen. Because those skills are unlikely to be readily transferable assets, economic rents will be earned by better fishermen, even under open access conditions in the fishery.

Although there are incentives for fishermen to organize for both private and governmental restrictions on harvest, these catch or yield differences among fishermen will affect the kinds of agreements that can be reached privately and the cohesiveness of political lobby groups for molding formal regulations. With the differential rents that exist when fishermen are heterogeneous, some fishermen may have a stake in maintaining current conditions in the fishery and in opposing regulatory change, if it seriously upsets status quo rankings and redistributes income.

To illustrate the potential distributional impact of various regulatory policies and how political bargaining lines might be drawn, consider limited access schemes. These arrangements go beyond season closures, whereby access to the fishery is limited to set periods of time. Unless augmented by other controls on individual fishing effort or catch, season closures may have only a small impact on rent dissipation because of open entry during the fishing season and the corresponding rush to fish. Limited access policies usually involve issuing a restricted number of fishing licenses and allowing entry only to licensees as a means of reducing overall harvest rates and pressure on the stock of fish. With the number of licenses kept small relative to the number of fishermen who would fish under open access conditions and entry restricted to license holders, rents can be increased. If the licenses are considered to be a permanent assignment of access to the fishery and are transferable, they can become a valuable property right to fish.

Because of the potential wealth assignment involved, determining who will receive the initial licenses and the procedure by which they will be granted will be important problems to be resolved. Political influence, based on numbers, cohesion, and wealth, will likely be a more critical determinant of who receives licenses than will be other criteria, such as the impact of various fishing groups on fishery rents. Although fishing licenses, as such, were not involved in early regulation in the Pacific Northwest salmon fishery, the success of the more numerous sports and commercial fishermen, who used high-cost mobile gear, is denying access to the fishery to the owners of lower-cost fish wheels and fish traps illustrates the role of political influence in shaping regulatory policies.[4] Because total rents can be increased and redistributed through licensing arrangements, some fishermen therefore can be made better off relative to their position in the status quo. Within the group receiving licenses, however, the problems of designing and enforcing *intragroup* controls on fishing remain in order to avoid rent dissipation along other margins.

Some of the equal access questions that may be politically important can be resolved if *transferable* licenses are granted to some incumbent fishermen, perhaps through a lottery. Under that arrangement, a market could develop for the exchange of licenses to allow new fishermen to enter or to allow some of those who were excluded to reenter the fishery. The transfer of licenses, however, can involve other problems that could affect how fishermen perceive the benefits from adopting a limited access licensing program. For example, incumbent skilled fishermen could have their catch reduced by the exchange of licenses among other parties. If a less skilled fishermen sold his license to a more skilled new entrant, total fishing effort and harvest could increase and reduce average yields. In that case, even the incumbent fisherman who was not party to the transaction could be made worse off by the transfer of the license. In general, uncertainty over the details of limited entry schemes, such as conditions for transferability, can contribute to dissension and raise the political costs of establishing the program.

Another important detail that will affect the support of fishermen for limiting entry is the procedure by which licenses will be assigned. If the licenses are granted by the government to some incumbent fishermen, the recipients will receive a wealth transfer. Politicians, however, may decide that a tax on the value of the license is warranted, perhaps to compensate those who are excluded from the fishery. Similarly, if the licenses are sold by the government and perfect price discrimination is used, the government may extract all of the rents so that fishermen are no better off with the regulation. In either case, the adoption of taxes or pricing policies in limited access schemes can reduce the welfare gain to fishermen from the new program and sharply reduce their enthusiasm for it.

It was noted above that rent dissipation can still be substantial with limited licensing, unless controls are placed on the catch or effort of those fishermen who hold licenses. One way to address this problem is for the regulatory agency to set a total allowable catch within the fishery and to

[4]Similarly, in 1982–83 in response to perceived declines in the stock of redfish, the Texas legislature adopted regulations that prohibited commercial fishing of redfish in Texas. Importantly, the legislation allowed more numerous sports fishermen to continue to harvest redfish.

allocate and enforce catch quotas among the licensed fishermen. Individual transferable quotas are an attractive option because with eligible fishermen assigned a share of total allowable catch, there is less need for bureaucratic regulation of gear type, harvest season, and vessel size. With catch quotas, individual fishermen can make input decisions to maximize their returns with regulation focusing on the determination of total allowable catch and quota compliance. If quota arrangements are viewed as permanent, exclusive, and transferable, they become a limited property right to the stock, encouraging fishermen to engage in wealth-increasing behavior. But despite these attractions, agreement on the specifics of quota schemes may be difficult. Because individual catch quotas can involve a long-term assignment of wealth, competition for them is likely to be intense, and disputes over quota assignment may limit the formation of a unified collective effort among fishermen in political lobbying.

In addition to the question of who will receive quotas, there is the issue of how they will be assigned. One possibility is to devise quotas on the basis of past or historical catch. Another option is to grant uniform quotas. Quotas based on historical catch recognize and preserve the differential performance of skilled fishermen and will be preferred by them. Disputes, however, are likely over verification of historical differential yields. Newer entrants, who do not have historical catch records and who are learning by doing, will oppose grandfathering quotas on the basis of past performance. The alternative use of uniform quotas or equal shares avoids the verification problems associated with historical catch and address some of the concerns of newer fishermen. However, they could harm established, better-skilled fishermen by disproportionately constraining their catch. The purchase of transferable quotas from other less skilled fishermen may mitigate this effect, but nevertheless, skilled fishermen are likely to object that uniform quotas fail to recognize their greater productivity.

This discussion of the contracting problems underlying the adoption of individual transferable quotas assumes that they are seen by fishermen as permanent arrangements. Fishermen will have more difficulty in gauging the benefits of quotas and, hence, in supporting them if the quotas are seen as temporary or uncertain, as they may be. Uncertainty regarding the size of annual quotas, the duration of quota policies, and the nature of other regulatory actions will add to the difficulties facing fishermen in calculating individual benefits from the new arrangement relative to the status quo. Moreover, uncertain quotas may encourage fishermen to violate their allocations, raising enforcement costs and reducing the effectiveness of the policy in enhancing the growth of the stock and aggregate fishing incomes. Nevertheless, regulatory officials and politicians have some incentives to adopt temporary quotas. A permanent quota system could sharply reduce the administrative authority of regulators and justification for agency staffing and budgets. Further, permanent quotas limit the ability of politicians to respond to changing political demands for free access to the fishery. With transferable permanent quotas, subsequent exchanges of access rights will be through market transactions and not through political assignments. Finally, there will be political pressures opposing a permanent quota system from fishermen who have their access and harvest opportunities reduced as well as from input suppliers, ranging from fishing crews to vessel and equipment manufacturers and retailers, who have a stake in a less restrictive regulatory regime.

Even if quotas can be agreed to, they will not control all rent dissipation. Each fisherman has incentive to harvest early to fill his quota when fish stocks are high and costs are relatively lower. The resulting rush and investment in capital and labor inputs raise the aggregate costs of landing the allowable catch.

The distributional concerns surrounding the adoption of quota systems will be reduced and the opportunities for collective action by fishermen increased if the aggregate gains were very large, as might be the case if the fishery was so severely overfished that incomes or returns per unit of effort were very low. Additionally, quotas or other regulatory policies will be less costly to adopt if they are assigned in new fisheries, where there are no preexisting claims or historical catch differences that must be reconciled in the new system. This suggests that cohesive lobby pressure by fishermen for quotas and other arrangements to control individual fishing effort and catch are most likely in either very new or very depleted fisheries.

EMPIRICAL PREDICTIONS AND EVIDENCE

The previous discussion argued that disagreements over rental shares and the details of many regulatory schemes lead incumbent fishermen, politicians, and bureaucrats to favor general catch-enhancing policies that do not seriously upset status quo distributions and to avoid restrictions on individual fishing. However, increasing aggregate catch is only a short-term response to the common pool problem; it does not address the fundamental incentives of individuals to compete away fishing rents in the absence of property rights to the stock. Where conditions have deteriorated, reducing the number of fishermen and raising the aggregate gains from tighter controls, limited licensing, restrictions on total allowable catch, and individual transferable quotas may be considered for addressing common pool losses. This section examines empirical evidence regarding the informal and formal regulatory controls that have been implemented in various fisheries with special attention placed on the Gulf Coast shrimp fishery.

Informal contracting

One option for reducing common pool losses is the use of private group controls with possible enforcement by the government. Informal agreements similar to mining camp rules could provide for limited controls on effort and catch and could restrict entry by outsiders. More structured, private regulations through unions or trade associations could also restrain fishing by members and deny access to others. If successful, these arrangements could bring some relief from common pool losses. The extent of the gains, however, depends upon the type of rules adopted and enforcement.

Anthropological studies by Forman (1967), Breton (1977), and Cordell (1978), point out that local territorial fishing rights have been used frequently in many societies, but they tend to break down as competition for the resource increases and the ability of customs or behavioral norms to enforce local rules deteriorates. Further, these studies of informal fishing rules indicate that intragroup controls on individual effort or catch are quite limited. Acheson (1975) discusses the private agreements among Maine lobstermen to allocate territorial rights that are enforced by threats of violence. Nevertheless, his study suggests that many areas are not adequately defended and have common pool conditions. Wilson's (1977) study of the same locality indicates that enduring private agreements to assign territorial rights and limit fishing are absent in over 90 percent of the fishery. Finally, Bell's (1972) examination of the northern U.S. lobster fishery shows that where informal agreements among fishermen are forthcoming, they represent very incomplete responses to common pool problems. He estimates that greater efficiency could be achieved in the fishery with half of the observed level of effort. Similar results for informal regulations in the inshore Newfoundland cod fishery have been reported by Andersen and Stiles (1973), Andersen (1979), and Martin (1979). Although this discussion involves only a limited survey of a large and impressive literature on informal fishing practices, the evidence suggests that such institutions are most viable when fisheries are not subject to intense competition or when customary practices are recognized and enforced by the state.

In the United States, unions and trade associations appear to have offered a more structured alternative to informal agreements for restricting outsiders and for policing the compliance of members to fishing rules. Fishermen unions were particularly active along U.S. coasts in the 1930s through the 1950s. Because they generally were associations of skippers with crews paid on a share basis, these were not labor unions in the typical sense. They implemented policies to increase member incomes by limiting entry to those in the union and by negotiating price agreements with wholesalers and canneries. In some cases, the price agreements also had the important effect of restricting the catch of low-value, adolescent fish, allowing them to develop for subsequent, higher-valued harvest. The union could enforce these fishing rules. Union agreements, however, were dismantled by the federal government as violations of the Sherman Act due to complaints by excluded fishermen and by canners who preferred to negotiate prices with individual fishermen and not with an organized group that would have greater bargaining power in fixing local prices.[5]

The regulations adopted by the Gulf Coast Shrimpers' and Oystermen's Association as documented in the transcript of record for *The Gulf Coast Shrimpers' and Oystermen's Association v. U.S.*, 236 F.2d 658 (1956), indicate how that union addressed common pool problems, given the contracting problems described above. The union was organized in the 1930s to regulate shrimping and to set prices along the Mississippi coast. Practically all commercial shrimp and oyster fishermen operating from the five major ports in Mississippi were members. Under union rules, they were permitted to sell only at or above the association's floor price and to packers who agreed to its rules. Although the court found that the union was price fixing, an examination of the transcript of record for the case indicates that the actions of the union were designed also to impact the harvest practices of members.

Because shrimp is an annual crop, intensive harvest of small shrimp early in the season limits the number of larger, more valuable adults that will be available for catching later in the year. By fixing prices that were to be paid by packers to control the harvest of small, immature shrimp and by restricting entry to members, the union could provide some increase in member incomes, even though shrimp were sold in a national market. Minimum prices based on shrimp size (tails per pound) were established by the union and distributed among packers and members. By setting a minimum price for small shrimp that generally *exceeded* prices paid elsewhere for that class, the association reduced the quantity of small shrimp demanded by the packers. Indeed, testimony in the case

[5]Major cases include Columbia River Packers v. Hinton, 315 U.S. 520 (1942), Manaka v. Monterey Sardine Industries, 41 F. Supp. 531 (1941), Hawaiian Tuna Packers v. International Longeshoremen's and Warehousemen's Union, 72 F. Supp. 562 (1947), McHugh v. U.S., 230 F.2d 252 (1956), Local 36 of International Fishermen and Allied Workers of America et al. v. U.S., 177 F2d 320 (1949), and The Gulf Coast Shrimpers' and Oystermen's Association v. U.S., 236 F.2d 658 (1956).

indicates that whenever the market price for small shrimp fell below the union's floor price, as was frequent, packers temporarily closed down, and shrimpers stopped fishing. Accordingly, the higher price required for smaller shrimp acted to redirect harvest to later in the season and thereby increase the yield of higher-valued larger shrimp. The market price per pound for larger shrimp was at least double that for smaller shrimp, and union minimum prices for larger shrimp were generally *at or below* that market price.

The price-setting efforts of the union appear to have been augmented by the establishment in 1934 by the Mississippi state government of a legal minimum harvest size for shrimp of forty shrimp per pound. This size restriction was larger than the sixty-eight per pound required by neighboring Louisiana. The union was apparently an advocate of the minimum catch size limitation, and it attempted to enforce the rule. If shrimp smaller than the legal minimum were brought to a packing house, union peelers refused to peel them. To further enforce the size and price rules, the union required that all captains fishing for small shrimp carry a purchase contract from a packer at the association price. Fines and suspension from fishing were levied by the union on its members for failure to comply.[6]

The union's efforts to direct harvest to larger shrimp in Mississippi waters seemingly were successful. Average shrimp price data for Mississippi and Louisiana during the period 1948 through 1953 when the union was active indicate that Mississippi prices were higher due to the harvest of larger shrimp.[7] Louisiana shrimpers were attracted to the Mississippi fishery, but union members opposed this entry by outsiders. The union pressured Mississippi packers not to buy shrimp below the union price and to deny ice and fuel to nonunion shrimpers. Violent confrontations between union members and Louisiana shrimpers followed, as the union attempted to drive the Louisiana shrimpers from the Mississippi fishery. The Mississippi union apparently did not allow the Louisiana shrimpers to join in order to reserve the benefits of harvesting larger shrimp for members. This evidence from the *Gulf Coast Shrimper's* case suggests that the union was successful during the period that it

[6]Transcript of Record, Gulf Coast Shrimpers and Oystermen's Association v. United States, "Bylaws" of the Gulf Coast Shrimpers and Oystermen's Association, p. 11.

[7]As noted by Johnson and Libecap (1982), average shrimp price data from 1948, when data are first available, through 1953 in Mississippi and Louisiana show significant differences between the two states (U.S. Department of Commerce, Bureau of the Census, 1977). If Mississippi catch had a greater proportion of larger, more valuable shrimp, the average price would be higher. A one-tailed t test of the difference in the means of the ratios of Mississippi to Louisiana prices for 1948–53, and 1954–9 (the postunion period) shows that they are significantly different from zero at the 95 percent confidence level.

was allowed to operate in increasing the value of aggregate catch by restricting the harvest of immature shrimp and by denying access to nonmembers. The success of the union indicates that private group regulations of fisheries could be an alternative to government regulation if that option were politically acceptable. It is important to note, though, that there is no evidence that the union implemented controls on individual catch or effort or used other measures to allocate harvest among members. As discussed earlier, such internal controls involve the greatest controversies and dissension.

Formal regulation

The regulation of shrimp harvest by the Texas Parks and Wildlife Department in the bays and Gulf waters off Texas also is similar to the pattern of regulation described under "The Gains from Contracting and Bargaining Problems. Limited-entry regulations, such as restrictive licenses, to deny access to some fishermen and to lower total catch have not been adopted in the Texas shrimp fishery, even though average catch has fallen from its peak in 1963. *Unlimited* numbers of licenses are available for both the bay and Gulf shrimp fisheries with payment of fishermen and boat license fees. Although there are differential rates for resident and nonresident fishermen, the fees are sufficiently low so as not to be a barrier to entry. For example, 1988 commercial license fees are $15 for residents and $100 for nonresidents. Efforts were made by Texas fishermen in 1947 and 1949 to restrict access to the Texas fishery by out-of-state fishermen through much higher license fees and limits on the number of out-of-state licenses to be offered, but those efforts were rejected by the courts.[8]

Although no regulatory constraints on entry into the shrimp fishery have been adopted, there are regulations to increase the value of aggregate catch by protecting immature shrimp through season closures, gear restrictions, and minimum shrimp harvest size. As early as 1931, shrimpers supported season closures during nursery periods to allow small shrimp to develop. In 1941, shrimpers lobbied for the first coastwide spring season closure in inland waters. The 1959 Texas Shrimp Conservation Act defined specific harvest periods to protect small shrimp.

Shrimpers have agreed in principle to season closure, which are designed to expand the aggregate stock and do not discriminate in access during the open season, but conflicts have developed over access to

[8]In 1981, there were attempts by the bay shrimpers in Texas to formally limit entry into the bay shrimp fishery by denying new licenses. This unsuccessful effort was designed to block further entry by an outside group, Vietnamese fishermen, who were settling on the Texas coast.

particular kinds of immature shrimp. Beginning in the 1950s, two separate shrimp fisheries developed in Texas, based on the kind of shrimp of commercial importance to each. One was the bay fishery that focused largely on the white shrimp that developed in the spring and remained as adults in the bays. The 1959 Shrimp Conservation Act defined an open fall season in the bays from August 15 through December 15 for harvesting mature white shrimp by bay fishermen. The second shrimp fishery in the Gulf of Mexico where shrimpers harvested adult brown shrimp that also developed in the bays in the spring but, unlike white shrimp, migrated as juveniles to the Gulf.

Bay shrimpers had incentive to agree to seasons that protected immature white shrimp, because they had access to them as adults. On the other hand, bay shrimpers did not have the same incentive to protect immature brown shrimp, which migrated to the deep waters of the Gulf of Mexico and were harvested by Gulf shrimpers. In the bay nurseries brown and white shrimp tended to be in different areas so that bay shrimpers could harvest small brown shrimp while minimizing the catch of young white shrimp.

Gulf shrimpers opposed this practice because it reduced the number of shrimp that could successfully migrate to the Gulf. In 1959, Gulf shrimpers succeeded in lobbying the Texas legislature to close the bay fishery in the spring from March 1 to July 15 to allow brown shrimp to develop. The Gulf also was closed from June 1 through July 15 for the same reason. Bay shrimpers opposed the spring closing of the bays, and they succeeded in amending the Shrimp Conservation Act in 1963 to allow for a limited spring season from May 15 through July 15. Nevertheless, political conflict has continued between the two groups as the Gulf fishery has continued to lobby to close the spring season in the bays.

Although shrimpers generally have not agreed to internal effort controls, bay shrimpers have accepted gear restrictions on minimum net mesh size. These reinforce the effect of season closures by allowing small shrimp to escape the pull of nets. They also have supported other limits on the number and size of nets that can be used in the bays. During the fall adult white shrimp season, only one net twenty-five feet in width can be pulled by any vessel. This restriction is not designed to limit the harvest of bay shrimpers, but rather to reduce the incentive of larger Gulf vessels to enter the bays during the fall season. Because the more powerful Gulf vessels could pull multiple large nets and out compete small bay vessels, the restriction is used to reduce the competitive advantage of Gulf vessels over inshore boats. There are no restrictions on the number or size of trawl nets used in the Gulf.

The conflict between Gulf and bay shrimpers over the harvest of immature shrimp also has led to the imposition of individual catch limits on bay shrimpers during the spring brown shrimp season. Daily limits of 300 pounds per vessel have been assigned in the bays in the spring, but *no* catch restrictions are imposed for fall bay white shrimp season or the fall and winter brown shrimp season in the Gulf. Taxes and other internal effort controls have received little political support from shrimpers and have not been adopted.

SUMMARY

The apparent inability of fishermen to biologically overfish the shrimp fishery, even though catch per unit of effort has fallen, has prevented conditions from deteriorating to a level that would lead to political agreements among shrimpers, regulators, and politicians in Texas on more restrictive controls on individual effort to reduce common pool losses. Instead as suggested under "The Gains from Contracting and Bargaining Problems," the regulations that have received support are those that are designed to increase aggregate catch with little or no impact on shares, such as seasons and related equipment restrictions. Shrimpers also have been able to agree on regulations that are designed to limit the fishing of *rivals* as indicated in the conflict between bay and Gulf shrimpers. So long as the stock of shrimp is maintained through annual recruitment, reducing the pressure for stricter regulation of access and of individual catch in the Texas shrimp fishery, a suboptimal political equilibrium may persist, whereby incomes remain low for a large number of shrimpers and rents are dissipated through excessive labor and capital investment.

This discussion of fisheries emphasizes the importance of the details of contracting for property rights for determining how a society responds to common pool losses. For many fisheries the institutional solutions have been very incomplete and serious rent dissipation has continued. Understanding the chronic nature of problems such as these requires further analysis of the distributional conflicts that hinder the adoption of more complete property rights. Chapter 6 continues this investigation of contracting for property rights to reduce the losses of the common pool by examining competitive crude oil extraction.

6

Contracting for the unitization of oil fields

INTRODUCTION

This chapter examines the contracting problems encountered in efforts to unitize the production of crude oil in the United States. Since the first discovery of petroleum in the United States in 1859, oil production has been plagued by serious common pool losses. These losses arise as numerous firms compete for migratory oil lodged in subsurface reservoirs. Under the common law rule of capture, private property rights to oil are assigned only upon extraction. This follows similar practices in allocating property rights to other naturally occurring resources, such as fish, wildlife, and even frontier federal land. For each of the firms on a reservoir, a strategy of dense-well drilling and rapid production allows it to drain oil from its neighbors and to take advantage of the low extraction costs that exist early in field development. In new, flush oil fields, subsurface pressures are sufficient to expel the oil without costly pumping or injection of water or natural gas into the reservoir to drive oil to the surface.

Under these conditions, when there are multiple firms on a reservoir, each firm has incentive to drill competitively and drain to increase its share of oil field rents, even though these individual actions lead to aggregate common pool losses. Rents are dissipated as capital costs are driven up with the drilling of excessive numbers of wells (more than geologic conditions require or price and interest rate projections warrant) and with the construction of surface storage, where the oil can be held safe from drainage by other firms. Unfortunately, once in surface storage, oil is vulnerable to fire, evaporation, and spoiling. Rapid extraction also increases production costs as subsurface pressures are vented prematurely, forcing the early adoption of pumps and injection wells. Total oil recovery falls as pressures decline because oil becomes trapped in surrounding formations, retrievable only at very high extraction costs.

Finally, rents are dissipated as production patterns diverge from those that would maximize the value of output over time.

There never has been much disagreement over either the nature of the common pool problem or the general solution to it. Early discussions of restrained oil production in the United States emphasized extraordinary wastes. In 1910, oil losses from fire and evaporation from surface storage (wooden tanks or behind earthen dams) in California, a major producing state, ranged from 4 to 8 million barrels, or 5 to 11 percent of the state's production. In 1914, the director of the Bureau of Mines estimated losses from excessive drilling at $50 million, when the value of U.S. production was $214 million (Ise, 1926, pp. 91, 141; American Petroleum Institute, 1951, p. 166). In 1926, the Federal Oil Conservation Board (1926, p. 30; 1929, p. 10) estimated oil recovery rates of only 20 to 25 percent with competitive extraction, whereas recovery rates of 85 to 90 percent were thought possible with controlled withdrawal.

In 1928, competitive drilling on the Hendrick field of West Texas led to one well per ten acres at a cost of $57,000 per well, where porous geologic conditions suggested that only one well per eighty acres would have been sufficient to rapidly drain the reservoir. The associated loss in underground pressure forced premature oil pumping at a marginal cost of $.10 per barrel. Moderate withdrawal would have maintained pressure and allowed oil to flow *without pumping* until late in the field's life (*Oil Weekly,* March 23, 1928; April 13, 1928). Moreover, storage capacity was driven up by the competition for oil. During the first five months of 1928, storage capacity on the Hendrick field rose from 5,251,000 to 10,987,000 barrels at a cost of $3,842,300. By contrast, on the neighboring and similarly sized Yates field, where private controls limited production, storage was only 783,000 barrels at a cost of $274,000 (*Oil Weekly,* February 24, 1928; March 23, 1928; May 25, 1928). In 1937, the American Petroleum Institute estimated that unnecessary wells on the East Texas field cost over $200 million (American Bar Association, 1938, p. 256). In 1980, intensive drilling under prevailing ownership and regulatory practices in the United States left the United States with 88 percent of the world's oil wells and only 14 percent of the world's production (*International Petroleum Encyclopedia,* 1982, pp. 334–35).[1]

There also are pecuniary losses associated with competitive common pool extraction, because oil cannot be held in the reservoir in response to price and interest rate forecasts. With rapid competitive production, oil is dumped onto the market by firms, depressing prices. For example, be-

[1]For a general discussion of the costs of common pool oil production and the contractual alternatives facing firms, see Libecap and Wiggins (1984).

tween 1926 and 1930 there was an unprecedented clustering of oil field discoveries in the midcontinent region of the United States. These discoveries involved some of the largest fields ever discovered in North America, including the Seminole and Oklahoma City fields in Oklahoma and the Howard-Glasscock, McElroy, Van, Hendrick, Yates, and East Texas fields in Texas. Thousands of firms (many of them very small, organized to exploit single leases) were involved in developing those fields, prior to the general establishment of state-imposed regulatory controls. Between 1925 and 1929 U.S. crude oil production rose by 32 percent and prices fell (U.S. Department of Commerce, Bureau of the Census, 1975, p. 588). Before the discovery of the Seminole field in July 1926, the nominal midcontinent price for 36 gravity crude oil was $2.29 per barrel. Within a year, as crude oil supplies rose, the price fell to $1.28 per barrel (*Oil Weekly,* October 22, 1926). With additional output from the other fields, particularly the huge Oklahoma City and East Texas fields, prices fell to $.18 per barrel by July 1931.[2]

Although the common pool problem and its costs were long recognized in the industry, so was the most complete solution to it: fieldwide unitization. Both the Federal Oil Conservation Board and the American Institute of Mining and Metallurgical Engineers issued various reports in the 1920s and early 1930s on the merits of unitization.[3] Under unitization, production rights are delegated through negotiation to a single firm, the unit operator, with net revenues apportioned among all parties on the field (including those that would otherwise be producing). As the only producer on the field and a residual profit claimant, the unit operator has incentive to maximize field rents. Accordingly, unitization results in important economic gains: a time stream of output that more closely approximates the rent-maximizing pattern, increased oil recovery, and reduced wells and other capital costs. For instance, the *Oil Weekly* (April 13, 1942; May 3, 1943) estimated that early unitization of oil fields (gas solution) would increase recovery from two to five times that of unconstrained production. Similarly, on the Fairway field in Texas, the *Oil and Gas Journal* (December 7, 1964) predicted that unitization would increase oil recovery by 130 million barrels.

Despite these attractions for mitigating the substantial losses in

[2]The 79 percent fall in crude oil prices from $1.29 to $.18 between 1930 and 1931 greatly exceeded the 9 percent fall in general prices during that period (U.S. Department of Commerce, Bureau of the Census, 1975, p. 211).

[3]See, for example, the beneficial effects of unitization outlined by H. L. Doherty and others to the Federal Oil Conservation Board (1926, pp. 16–75). See, also, the Committee of Nine report on unitization Federal Oil Conservation Board (1929, Appendix A). An example of the discussions of unitization in the *Transactions of the AIME* is in American Institute of Mining and Metallurgical Engineers (1930, Vol. 86, pp. 11–121).

volved in common pool crude oil production, complete fieldwide unitization has not been widespread. Bain (1947, p. 29) noted: "It is difficult to understand why in the United States, even admitting all obstacles of law and tradition, not more than a dozen pools are 100 percent unitized (out of some 3,000) and only 185 have even partial unitization." Similarly, Libecap and Wiggins (1985) reported that as late as 1975 only 38 percent of Oklahoma production and 20 percent of Texas production came from fieldwide units.

Just why this is so is the subject of this chapter. The key issue in blocking agreement on the voluntary unitization of oil fields is conflict over a share formula to divide the net proceeds of unit production among the various parties. An early student of unitization, Williams (1952, pp. 1173–74), commented:

> "The principal obstacle to full, voluntary agreement is the problem of dividing the proceeds of production. If development of the area sought to be unitized is incomplete, there is a certain amount of gamblers' instinct to be overcome; some lessors and leasees may be inclined to rely on the possibility that their interests lie in the most favorable part of the producing structure and to take their chances that the entire production from their land will be more valuable than an undivided interest in production from a much larger unitized tract. If development of the pool is relatively complete, there is frequently acrimony as to the respective shares of production to be given owners with interests in favorable parts of the structure and owners of interests in less favorable areas.

This chapter examines the source of these distributional conflicts over unit shares. Uncertainties and information asymmetries regarding the valuation of individual firm oil leases, which are the basis for unit shares, are important contributors to the disagreements that block unitization, even in the presence of large and uncontroversial aggregate gains from unit formation. More than for any of the other cases examined in this volume, sufficient information is available for unitization to analyze the details of private contracting and the problems encountered in attempting to reach agreement. The discussion draws from Libecap and Wiggins (1985) and Wiggins and Libecap (1985).

THE CONTRACTING ENVIRONMENT

Oil reservoirs are commonly found below numerous independently owned surface tracts. The surface landowners initially hold the mineral rights, but transfer them to firms through mineral leases. By this process, multiple firms gain access to the pool, and the lease, rather than the field, becomes the unit of production. Many firms, particularly major producers, obtain multiple leases on a reservoir and have operations on many fields. In the United States with fragmented surface land ownership and tiny leases, many more firms, however, are very small with only a few leases on a single reservoir.

Typically, oil reservoirs are compressed between an upper layer of natural gas and a lower layer of water. The two layers, as well as gas dissolved in the oil, drive the oil to the surface when the surrounding formation is punctured by a well. Oil migrates to the well, draining neighboring areas. The extent of migration depends upon subsurface pressures, oil viscosity, and the porosity of the surrounding rock. Reservoirs are not uniform. These characteristics differ across the field, generating inherent variation in well productivity. As a firm drills additional wells, oil migrates more rapidly into the created low pressure zone, raising the firm's share of field output. Increases in the rate of production by any one firm, however, reduce ultimate aggregate oil recovery. With high withdrawal rates associated with competitive, common pool production, the ratio of natural gas and water to oil production increases, leading to a greater loss of subsurface reservoir pressure. As subsurface pressures decline, any gas dissolved in the petroleum goes out of solution. Because it is lighter and travels more quickly, the natural gas is expelled first, leading to a further fall in pressure per barrel of oil produced.

For example, on the Kelly-Snyder field in Texas, extraction on numerous leases between 1947 and 1952 led to a 46 percent drop in subsurface pressure from 3,122 to 1,675 pounds per square inch and a corresponding rise in gas/oil ratios from 870 to 1,163 cubic feet per barrel. This drop in pressure brought concern about the long-term viability of the Kelly-Snyder field, one of the largest in Texas (*Oil and Gas Journal,* March 26, 1962). With the loss of pressure and dissolved gas, oil becomes more viscous, clogging pore spaces in the reservoir and requiring more pressure to move it. Pockets of oil become trapped and are retrievable only with high extraction costs, including the premature need for artificial pumping or reinjection of water or gas to drive the oil to the surface.

To avoid common pool losses from competitive extraction on individual leases, firms have sought to unitize production through private agreement. With unitization, only one firm would develop the field, and the net returns would be distributed among all the relevant parties based on a predesignated sharing formula. The central issue in unitization contracting is agreement on an allocation formula for assigning unit revenues and costs among firms. Shares are based on estimates of each firm's contribution to the unit.

In share negotiations two serious problems arise. First, unitization contracts must assign once-and-for-all shares at the time the contract is completed. This is because changes in reservoir dynamics after unitization make it impossible to link unit production to particular leases, which would be necessary for adjusting shares. Before unitization, extraction occurs from each productive lease; but after unitization, the production pattern is fundamentally altered. The field, not the lease, is the producing unit, and wells are placed to maximize aggregate field returns. Many existing wells are plugged or used solely for injection of water, natural gas, or other substances to drive the oil to the unit's producing wells. These policies change the flow of oil migration in the reservoir, and the lease as a producing unit loses its significance. Postunitization production, then, cannot be used to infer relative lease values.

A second problem in unitization contracting is general uncertainty and asymmetrical information regarding relative preunitization lease values, which determine unit shares. These problems block agreement on lease value estimates and proposed shares in unit rents. The level of information available to the contracting parties depends upon the stage of production in which contracting occurs. In exploration, little is known regarding the location of oil and its commercial extraction possibilities. At that time, all leases are relatively homogeneous, and unitization agreements are comparatively easy to reach, using simple allocation formulas, often based on surface acreage. Since no party knows whether the formula is to its particular advantage or disadvantage, negotiators can focus on the aggregate gains from unitization.

Information problems and distributional concerns, however, arise with development, as oil reserves are proved and expanded. With the initial discovery well and the drilling of subsequent wells, lease heterogeneities emerge. Because reservoirs are not uniform, the information released from a well is descriptive of only the immediate vicinity. Hence, through drilling their individual leases, firms gain knowledge of their portion of the reservoir; the full extent of the deposit and the productive potential of other areas of the reservoir will be revealed only through the drilling activities of other firms.

The production potential and commercial value of a lease are functions of both public and private data. Public data include objectively measured and noncontroversial variables, such as the number of wells on the lease, its surface acreage, and the record of current and past production. These data are available to all of the contracting parties. Private data on lease parameters involve more subjective geological variables, which tend to be assessed and valued by individual company engineers. They include the amount of oil below lease lines – gross acre-feet of pay (volume of the producing formation), net acre-feet of pay (nonporous and non–oil-bearing rock is subtracted from gross acre-feet), remaining reserves (original oil in place less cumulative production), net oil migration, oil viscosity, permeability of the surrounding medium, and bottom hole pressure. These latter variables, which are important for assessing lease values, are a major source of contracting problems.

Information about them and their significance for lease value estimations are drawn from well logs and production histories. They require highly subjective interpretation by company engineers and geologists; estimations regarding them and their impact on unit shares, therefore, become very controversial. For an example of the disputes that can arise over the interpretation of these data, it was noted during negotiations in the Western RKM unit in Texas that "the Engineering Committee could not agree upon oil reserves for a large number of tracts in the unit area because of the poor quality and interpretive nature of the available basic data" (letter, March 13, 1963; Western RKM Unit File, company records).[4]

Although it is difficult to achieve consensus among firms on the implications of such information for lease values, these subsurface variables are nonetheless used by each firm to form private estimates of the value of its leases. The estimation of static reservoir characteristics, such as thickness and porosity, further illustrates the information problems that can lead to divergences between lease value calculations based on public data and those based on private information. Each calculation is based on only a small number of observations at well bores. The interpolation of the reservoir's structure between wells, however, is sensitive to the specific functional forms employed by company engineers. Procedures and estimates vary across firms. For instance, in unit negotiations on the Prentice field in West Texas there were differences in porosity estimates of 60 to 100 percent.

The estimation of dynamic reservoir characteristics, such as remaining oil reserves and future lease output, involves even greater complications. Companies often have differing opinions about the correct estimation procedure, when choices may reallocate millions of dollars. There is no generally accepted standard. The result of subjective estimates and differences in procedures is that consensus often cannot be achieved among the bargaining parties on future least output. Such an agreement, however, is necessary for successful unit share negotiations.

As a result of these problems, negotiations over the formation of oil field units must necessarily focus on a small set of objectively measurable variables, such as cumulative output or wells per acre, because of the

[4]The company records are from one of the largest oil producing firms in the United States. Libecap and Wiggins were granted access to unitization files on the condition of confidentiality. These files include letters, memorandums, minutes, recorded votes, engineering committee reports and other detail documents on contracting for unitization on each of the seven fields examined in this chapter.

potential disputes over the use of subsurface parameters. These objective measures, however, may be poor indicators of lease value. The resulting asymmetry in lease value calculations based on differential information and interpretation among firms is the primary cause of breakdown in unit share negotiations.

In addition to the problems of estimating static and dynamic geological characteristics, firms have other proprietary information that contributes to conflict over lease value estimates. Lease production is influenced by firm management policies, the details of which are available only from company records. Although company records are available to the firm's engineers and geologists, they can be misrepresented easily and may not be considered reliable by other firms. For example, in efforts to organized the North Cowden unit, one large firm noted that

> the validity of the selection of the pay is very interpretive, being dependent upon the individual who observed the drilling samples on that well . . . a disadvantage [of gross pay] is that we are basing a parameter of unitization on the skill or lack of skill in the persons observing the samples. Therefore, there is considerable question as to the consistency of the picks [estimates] between wells, and it would likely be difficult to reach an agreement between operators on such data. (letter, June 16, 1959; North Cowden Unit File, company records)

Thus, there are important differences in the data for estimating lease values and unit shares in negotiations. These differences inhibit agreement between the lease owner and other firms on the formation of a unit, even when there are large aggregate gains from such action. These conflicts over lease values and unit shares will continue until late in the life of a reservoir. With the accumulation of information released through development and production, public and private lease value estimates converge as primary production (production based on natural subsurface pressure) approaches zero. At that point a consensus on shares and the formation of the unit is possible. Without artificial injection of natural gas or other substances to supplement underground pressure and other secondary recovery techniques, lease values will approach zero. Secondary recovery generally requires coordinated actions across multiple leases and, hence, is most effective with a unit. This suggests that as with fisheries, unit agreements are more likely to be reached late in the life of the reservoir. Unfortunately, by the time secondary recovery is required, most of the common pool losses already have occurred.

In unit negotiations, each of the bargaining parties compares the expected value of its returns under the status quo or nonunitized production with the expected value of returns with unitization, based on its offered share in the unit. The status quo returns are net of the firm's share of common pool losses, if the unit is not formed at that time. If the firm's private information indicates that the organizing committee's estimates of its lease values, based on public information, are too low, the firm may delay joining the unit. The decision will be based, in part, on whether the firm expects future production data to confirm its private value estimates and justify an upward revision in its unit share. The firm will also be concerned as to whether this gain in unit share offsets its portion of reservoir damage from delaying the unit. In addition to delaying because of conflicts based on information asymmetries, the firm also may decide to delay joining if it can obtain concessions from other parties by holding out. In the meantime, nonunitized production shares are determined by relative lease production capabilities, subject to any constraints imposed by regulatory authorities.[5]

The central factor, then, affecting a firm's probability of withholding its leases in anticipation of subsequent share increases is uncertainty regarding the public estimates of lease value used to assign unit shares. The most productive, longest-lived leases on a field are most apt to be withheld because they are subject to the greatest uncertainty regarding value. Those leases are more likely to be affected by future changes in subsurface conditions and, accordingly, have greater variance in lease value estimates and a higher probability of large divergence between public and private values. To estimate a lease's future producing capacity, it is necessary to have observations of the rate of production decline for its wells, which varies substantially across leases. On highly productive leases, which have not yet gone into decline, such observations will not be available for unit negotiations. Hence, estimates must be made as to the timing and rate of production decline, based on the subjective opinions of engineers and geologists, and these opinions will be open to dispute.

This suggests that all things equal, firms with very productive leases will be less likely to join a unit. The size of a firm's holdings on a field, however, will affect its decision to withhold productive leases from the unit. For firms with large leased acreage, the gains from delaying the unit because of disputes over the value of one lease are likely to be more than offset by losses on other leases. If so, this reduces the probability that delaying the unit until more public information is available will bring a sufficiently large increase in rental share to compensate for the damage to the firm's other leases. On the other hand, for smaller firms with limited

[5]Regulatory arrangements in the absence of unitization are outlined in Libecap and Wiggins (1984).

field acreage, these aggregate reservoir effects are largely external. Those small firms (based on limited leased acreage) have greater incentive to withhold their highly productive leases, which have high variance in value estimates. If the acreage of firms with larger, multiple leases is in contiguous leases, then in the presence of continuing disagreements over unit shares, the firm may decide to leave negotiations and form a subunit on part of the field. As shown below, however, subunits, although preferable to no unitization, involve significantly higher costs and lower returns than do complete units.

Besides the information issues that particularly affect the owners of small productive leases, these small firms have had other reasons for opposing unitization. As described later, small lease owners were given preferential drilling permits by regulatory authorities under prorationing controls adopted by states in the absence of widespread unitization. Those policies allowed such leases to be more densely drilled than larger leases, and with more wells per acre, small lease owners could drain neighboring areas. In unit negotiations, small lease owners, as vested interests in prorationing regulation, insist on protecting their regulation-imposed advantages in the unit allocation rule as a condition for joining. Differences in lease value estimates can block consensus on any side payments to draw potential holdouts into agreement. Under unanimity voting rules, small firms could delay or block the formation of fieldwide units.

EMPIRICAL EVIDENCE

The contracting arguments outlined in the previous section can be applied to seven Texas and New Mexico units for which information is available for detailed analysis: North Cowden, Goldsmith/Landreth, Prentice Northeast, Western RKM, Slaughter Estate, Empire Abo, and Goldsmith/San Andres. Table 6.1 summarizes the data and shows that in each of the cases, unitization contracting was a long process, requiring from four to nine years from the time negotiations began until agreements could be reached. Moreover, in five of the seven cases the acreage in the final unit was less than that involved in the early negotiations. Overviews of negotiations on three of the fields illustrates the private contracting issues encountered in attempting to form units.

The North Cowden field was discovered in 1930, but negotiations for the unit did not begin until 1958 as the field neared depletion of primary reserves. An engineering committee was formed by the negotiating parties to collect field and lease data from the various operators to assign shares to the unit and to estimate the aggregate gains from secondary recovery under the proposed unit. Two years later in 1960, the

Table 6.1 *Unit contracting summaries for seven fields*

Field	Discovery date	Date unit negotiations began	Date unit formed	Acreage under negotiations	Acreage in final unit
North Cowden	1930	1958	1966	30,870	17,503
Goldsmith/Landreth	NA[a]	1961	1965	10,760	8,985[b]
					7,815
Prentice Northeast	1951	1954	1963	8,500	6,828
Western RKM	NA	1962	1966	16,400	4,918
Slaughter Estate	NA	1958	1963	5,528	5,280
Empire Abo	1957	1965	1971	11,323	11,323
Goldsmith/San Andres	NA	1959	1963	7,199	6,103

[a]*Note:* NA, not available
[b]*Note:* Separate reservoirs.

Source: Adapted from Wiggins and Libecap (1985).

committee produced estimates that oil recovery would increase by 100 million barrels with unitization, a gain of $285 million in 1960 prices (minutes, July 28, 1960; North Cowden Unit File, company records). Despite these prospective aggregate gains, nineteen of the thirty-one firms on the field eventually withdrew part or all of their leased acreage from the proposed unit, and a smaller unit was not formed until 1966, eight years after negotiations began.

Contracting for the Goldsmith/Landreth unit began in 1961, but conflict over unit boundaries delayed work by the engineering committee until 1963. With the assembled field and lease data, unit revenues and firm shares were estimated and presented for discussion. In the ensuing negotiations four of the ten firms bargaining for the unit withdrew their leases in disagreement over the proposed allocation rules. Additionally, after a share formula was finally agreed upon, another firm withdrew eight more leases due to a dispute over unit secondary recovery plans. The final smaller unit was not formed until October 1965.

The Prentice field was discovered in 1951, and unit negotiations began in 1954. Despite predictions that early unitization would substantially increase oil recovery, negotiations faltered and were abandoned between 1956 and 1959. In 1959, the largest firm on the field attempted to reopen negotiations, but by 1963, it was clear that fieldwide unitization was not possible. In late 1963, three subunits were formed, nearly ten years after initial negotiations because "a common formula could not be negotiated" (minutes, Operators' Meeting, February 7, 1963; Prentice Northeast Unit File, company records).

There is clear evidence that the very productive leases were systematically withheld from early unitization efforts on the seven fields, even though there were large and generally undisputed aggregate gains from fieldwide unitization. On the North Cowden field, firms with very productive leases voiced opposition to the proposed unit in early negotiations, with one firm asserting that "none of the proposed parameters give justice to those leases because of the abnormal producing capabilities" (letters, January 20, 1959; March 30, 1961; North Cowden Unit File, company records). Eight of the firms that eventually withdrew acreage from the proposed unit had ten of the most productive leases on the field. During the first six months of 1960, output from those leases averaged 133 barrels per acre, while the average for all other leases on the field was 79 barrels per acre (engineering report, December 1, 1960; North Cowden Unit File, company records). In negotiations one of the unit proponents reported: "It is extremely difficult to arrive at a single factor which can be said to represent an equitable minimum, since the field is currently under active development and current production relationships are changing with each month's data" (letter, February 5, 1960; North Cowden Unit File, company records).

In unit discussions, firms with small productive leases repeatedly demanded changes in the proposed unit allocation formulas. For example, on the Goldsmith/Landreth field, three firms with unusually productive leases requested that acreage be deleted from any allocation rule. Those three firms had leases with average output per acre three times that for other leases on the field and would have been disadvantaged by any share formula that considered surface acreage as an allocation parameter.

On the Goldsmith/San Andres field, in votes on various share formulas none of the firms consistently voting no had over 9 percent of productive field acreage. On the other hand, the three largest firms with 26, 16, and 15 percent of total acreage, respectively, voted yes on *all* of the allocation rules submitted for consideration. The small firms on the field repeatedly called for adjustments in the weights placed on specific parameters to reflect their individual advantages. One firm with 5 percent of field acreage, but only 1 percent of cumulative output, called for less weight to be placed on cumulative output, while another with 4 percent of acreage, but only 2.8 percent of current output, wanted current production removed or discounted in share formula calculation (minutes, January 10, 12, 1962; February 7, 1962; Goldsmith/San Andres Unit File, company records).

Available evidence also supports the notion that firms with large holdings on a given field will be the agents of institutional change. The motivation of large firms to promote fieldwide unitization is reflected in the following statement regarding a feared increase in unit costs due to the withdrawal of some leases from the proposed unit: "Although our reserves in the area from which all eleven tracts are eliminated are indicated to be greater . . . , our costs will undoubtedly be greater due to the requirement of additional injection wells . . ." (letter, October 12, 1964; Goldsmith/Landreth Unit File, company records).

To promote agreement, firms with large acreage in proposed units tended to be more flexible in negotiations over allocation rules. For example, on Goldsmith/San Andres field, the larger operators with 72.23 percent of current output, agreed to a smaller aggregate share of 71.09 percent of remaining primary production under the unit and 67.80 percent of secondary recovery output (letter, October 27, 1961; Goldsmith/San Andres Unit File, company records).

On the other hand, if negotiations reached an impasse, those firms with large blocks of contiguous acreage could withdraw and form their own subunits, even though the gains were less than from fieldwide units. During the lengthy North Cowden unitization discussions, three firms with large tracts of contiguous acreage finally withdrew to form separate subunits, avoiding the need to reach a share agreement among all of the firms on the field. Similarly, in negotiations for the formation of a 26,000-acre RKM unit on the Slaughter field in Texas, conflicts over proposed sharing formulas led to the exit of many of the contracting firms. The second largest firm with 26 percent of field acreage concentrated in the eastern part of the field, withdrew to form a separate subunit, arguing that the parameters considered for share assignment "considerably under-estimated" its lease values (letter, May 20, 1964; Western RKM Unit File, company records). The final Western RKM subunit was only 4,918 acres in size.

The failure to agree to fieldwide units and the formation of subunits brought significant losses. The *Oil and Gas Journal,* June 17, 1957, estimated 44 percent recovery of original oil in place for fully unitized fields, but only a 39 percent recovery for partially unitized fields. On smaller subunits, secondary recovery methods are less effective than when the whole reservoir is involved. Besides lower overall recovery, partial unitization leads to increased capital costs. For instance, after the unsuccessful efforts to completely unitize the 71,000-acre Slaughter field in West Texas, ultimately 28 separate subunits were established; these ranged from 80 to 4,918 acres. To prevent migration of oil across subunit boundaries, some 427 offsetting water injection wells were sunk along each subunit boundary, at a cost per well of approximately $360,000 for a total of $156 million.[6] These wells and related expenses were not needed for production and could have been avoided with a fieldwide unit. Such practices have been routine, particularly in Texas where multiple units are common (*Oil and Gas Journal,* July 9, 1956; March 1, 1965).

It was argued earlier that the range of share parameters for allocating unit rents will be limited because they must be based upon publically available information. This limits contracting flexibility because of the small number of available variables and the highly tenuous and controversial nature of even modest extrapolations from them to estimate individual lease values. For example, early in unit negotiations the engineering committee on North Cowden reported that data were too sketchy to calculate "a fair and equitable" gross or net pay under each lease. The committee had well cores for only 28 of the 733 wells on the field, and it stressed the "meager data and poor quality of available records" (memo, April 7, 1959; North Cowden Unit File, company records). As a result, during the eight years of negotiations for the North Cowden unit, nearly all of the numerous share formulas considered were combinations of current and cumulative output, which were available and reliable for all leases. Attempts to incorporate more sophisticated parameters met with objection from the bargaining parties due to their subjective nature, given the lack of available data. Further, remaining oil reserves for the various leases could not be estimated in ways acceptable to all the firms. The major unit proponent had access to reservoir data and could have estimated the parameter, but its estimations would have been controversial. Instead, the firm chose to release the data to the engineering committee for parameter calculation. One small firm, however, hired an outside consultant to calculate its net reserves and received estimates that were double those calculated by the engineering committee (letters, January 9, 1962; March 8, 1963; North Cowden Unit File, company records).

On the Prentice Northeast field, the final accepted share formula for the unit included only one variable, current production. Estimates of another possible parameter, primary oil recovery for the leases, were made using a variety of techniques, but "relatively poor agreement between various methods were obtained in many instances. Primary reason for inconsistencies [was] due to a severe lack of control in much of

[6]Increased well costs on the Slaughter field of Texas due to the failure to agree on a fieldwide unit were calculated by counting the otherwise unnecessary injection wells along subunit boundaries as shown on Slaughter field maps (August 22, 1967, Western RKM Unit File, company records). Costs per well are from Slaughter Estate Unit File, company records.

basic data, together with inherent uncertainties involved in these type of calculations" (engineering committee minutes, December 11, 1962; letter, June 29, 1963; Prentice North East Unit File, company records).

Finally, the evidence supports the notion that as fieldwide primary production nears an end, unitization agreements become more likely. The incentive to agree to the unit grows because secondary oil recovery through artificial injection of water or other substances to expel remaining oil is more effective with unitization. In addition, by that time information asymmetries among the firms become less important as all leases near primary depletion. Negotiations on North Cowden took eight years, in part, because some of the field was newly developed, while other parts were sharply declining. Much of the conflict centered on differences between these new and older sections of the field and how much each should share in the unit. In withdrawing its lease from the unit, one firm notified the unit organizers that "the various parts of the field were simply so diverse that no one formula could satisfy everyone. We wish you every success in forming a unit in the center of the field where everything is more uniform" (letter, September 4, 1963; North Cowden Unit File, company records). Similarly, agreement on a proposed early unit on the Empire Abo field could not be achieved in 1967. At that time most leases on the field could produce at the maximum amount allowed by regulators. A unit contract for Empire Abo was not signed until four years later in 1971, when primary production had so declined that the value of all leases was approaching zero and new production could occur only with unitization and related secondary recovery techniques.

POLICY DIFFERENCES REGARDING UNITIZATION AND THEIR IMPACT

In the circumstances of large and continuing common pool losses in oil production and the industry's inability to privately complete unitization agreements early in the development of a reservoir, political pressures mounted for government intervention to promote unitization. Differences among large and small firms regarding their incentive to support unitization limited the effectiveness of the oil industry as a cohesive lobby group. Moreover, the policies adopted varied dramatically across political jurisdictions, due to political opposition from smaller firms, who resisted government-enforced unitization. This section examines unitization policies and politics on federal lands in Wyoming and on private lands in Oklahoma and Texas.

Of the three, federal policy is the most effective in promoting unitization because it encourages agreement during exploration, rather than after field development. The stage of oil production in which bargaining occurs is critical for contracting success. During exploration, there is little asymmetric information across bargaining parties regarding relative lease values to block agreement. On the other hand with field development, differential information about lease productivity emerges, and disputes arise over lease value and unit shares.

This point is important for Oklahoma and Texas, because, in contrast to the federal government, those states allow for unitization only after oil fields have been discovered and fully developed. In Oklahoma, these problems are mitigated by regulations that permit 63 percent of the parties to coerce other firms to join the unit. In Texas, however, unanimous agreement is required.

Federal and state policies

All private oil production rights on federal lands are assigned through the Mineral Leasing Act of 1920, as amended (30 U.S.C. sections 181–287). Firms can obtain leases for up to twenty years under the Mineral Leasing Act, but the aggregate leased acreage held by a firm cannot exceed 246,000 acres in any state. If firms agree to unitize their leases, however, the leases are automatically extended for the life of the unit, and they are exempt from the statutory acreage limit (30 U.S.C. section 226j). Unit plans are approved and actively monitored by the Bureau of Land Management. These provisions provide incentives for firms to unitize on federal lands.

On federal lands unitization typically occurs once a potentially productive geological formation is identified by a prospecting firm. Other firms with leases in the area are identified, and the overlying acreage is unitized for exploration. The cost and revenue-sharing formula among the firms is based on surface acreage, because subsurface characteristics and production potentials are not yet known. Once a unit agreement is reached, prospecting is performed by only one firm, which is selected by a majority vote. As oil is discovered, proven productive areas are segregated from unproven areas by the Bureau of Land Management. Leases in proven areas, called *participating areas,* continue to share in the returns from the unit on the previously determined allocation formula. No firm shares in the unit revenues until its leases are shown to be productive.[7]

Because federal policy encourages early exploratory units before commercial petroleum deposits have been found, it allows for large

[7]Data on federal policy are based on interviews conducted by Libecap and Wiggins with the Bureau of Land Management, North Central Region, Casper, Wyoming, May 1982.

potential gains from unitization.[8] Early units can restrict the total number of wells drilled and control the pace of production to conserve subsurface pressure and increase total oil recovery. In addition, production can be adjusted in response to price and interest rate forecasts. As noted earlier, on federal lands the allocation arrangements are preset early in field development before information uncertainties and asymmetries appear regarding the interpretation of particular lease characteristics. During exploration very little is known regarding subsurface conditions, so that individual bargaining positions can be relatively homogeneous with little discord. Because reservoir information is limited, firms do not have any *ex ante* expected advantages from natural geological conditions associated with their leases. Hence, a simple sharing rule based on surface acreage is possible. This is the key policy that separates federal regulation from practices in Oklahoma and Texas.

The federal government has incentive to encourage unitization. As the principal land owner in areas where its regulations apply, the federal government captures a significant share of the increased field rents that result from efficient development. The federal government receives both cash bonuses and royalties from the private firms that develop its leased acreage.

In Oklahoma, compulsory unitization on order of the Oklahoma Corporation Commission has been possible since 1947 if a majority of the lease owners, weighted by acreage, vote for unitization (1945 Oklahoma Session Laws at 162; 1951 Oklahoma Session Laws at 136). In Texas, on the other hand, *unanimous* agreement for the formation of a unit is required before it will be approved by the Texas Railroad Commission. Further, unlike the federal government, both states require that the field be fully developed before a unit can be approved. Such requirements rule out the use of exploratory units as is possible on federal lands and the use of simple allocation rules. Because conflicts over lease value increase with development, the Oklahoma and Texas requirements for full development prior to unitization make agreements more difficult. Given these policy differences, one would expect variation in the extent of unitization on federal lands and in Oklahoma and Texas.

Impact of policy differences

Table 6.2 summarizes the patterns of unitization in Oklahoma, Texas, and Wyoming, which are largely on federal lands, for selected years from 1948 to 1975. The data indicate sharp differences in the amount of unitized production across the three states, with Wyoming having 50

[8]For most federal units, unitization dates precede field discovery dates. Only on very old fields do discovery dates precede unitization.

Table 6.2 *Production from field-wide units as a share of total state output for selected years in Wyoming, Oklahoma, and Texas*

Year	Wyoming (%)	Oklahoma (%)	Texas (%)
1948	58	9	0
1950	51	10	1
1955	55	25	4
1960	64	24	7
1965	70	30	16
1970	67	35	14
1975	82	38	20

Source: Adapted from Libecap and Wiggins (1985).

percent of its production from fieldwide units as early as 1948, whereas the Oklahoma share was 9 percent and Texas had no production from fully unitized fields in that year. Those differences persisted through 1975.

Political contracting for unitization legislation

The observed policy differences among the federal government, Oklahoma, and Texas are due to a variation in the political strength of the firms that are opposed to private unitization. In the discussion above, information problems in share negotiations particularly affected the stands taken by small lease owners with very productive acreage on a reservoir. If those firms are small producers with little or no acreage on other fields that would benefit from unitization there, then they are likely to mobilize to resist government policies to force unitization through the adoption of majority voting rules. A majority-imposed allocation rule and forced minority membership in the unit clearly could make these small firms worse off relative to the status quo by reassigning property rights to field rents. As described below, as a legacy of past political agreements regarding property rights, small producers also had regulatory-imposed advantages that would lead them to oppose compulsory unitization. Accordingly, any government policies to promote unitization when private agreements failed depended critically on the political power of these small firms.

The federal government was able to adopt its comparatively effective unitization policies with no recorded political opposition, because there were relatively fewer small producers and leases on federal lands and they had less influence on federal policy than did the numerous small firms in Oklahoma and Texas. The federal government's unitization policies were added to its leasing practices in 1930 in response to rapid extraction and competitive production in the North Dome Kettleman Hills field on federal lands in California (*Oil and Gas Journal,* July 3, 1930).[9]

The number of small producers on federal lands was limited because leases were typically large. The Mineral Leasing Act of 1920 allowed individual leases of up to 2,560 acres for prospecting and 640 acres for production. The federal government reserved the mineral rights underlying its land and issued large leases, because it did not gain from strategic drilling, which often was practiced on private land as both leasors and leasees tried to encourage oil migration to their leases.

On private lands in Oklahoma and Texas, however, lease size was determined by land ownership, which was much more fragmented. Further, landowners often divided their lands into multiple leases to encourage rapid production and drainage. The result was that very small leases were common in Oklahoma and Texas. For example, on the Oklahoma City field in 1930, there were approximately 85 leases of less than 50 acres, 111 leases of 50 to 350 acres, and only 1 lease of 640 acres (*Oil Weekly,* September 25, 1930). The East Texas field was even more fragmented, with many leases under five acres. Moreover, the small leasees often had no other holdings. Consequently in Oklahoma and Texas, there were more very small producers, which would be concerned about the valuation of their leases in unit shares or benefited from favorable prorationing rules, than existed on federal lands.

The smooth adoption of unitization to reduce common pool losses on federal lands was not repeated in either Oklahoma or Texas. Small firms in those states resisted private unitization agreements and were the core of political opposition to government regulations promoting unitization. Because these producers were relatively homogeneous, numerous, and often aligned with small oil field service companies and small land owners, their lobby efforts were successful in delaying unitization legislation in Oklahoma and Texas. In the absence of unitization, larger firms lobbied for statewide prorationing of oil production to limit total output, minimum well-spacing rules, and the forced pooling of leases to reduce drainage and general losses from dense drilling. Forced pooling allowed small leases to be consolidated into larger tracts for drilling to reduce well densities. The enactment of this legislation in Oklahoma facilitated the subsequent adoption of compulsory unitization legislation by reducing the advantages offered by current regulation for small firms.

Oklahoma adopted formal minimum well-spacing rules and com-

[9]For discussion of the use of unitization on federal lands and the relationship to the famous Teapot Dome oil leases, see Libecap (1984).

pulsory lease pooling in 1935 and 1941, respectively (American Bar Association, 1938, pp. 209–10; Myers, 1967, p. 312). Spacing and compulsory pooling resulted in more uniform drilling on new fields and narrowed the advantages of small leases to only those arising from their natural position on the reservoir. Those policies helped to reduce opposition to compulsory unitization legislation in Oklahoma, which finally passed in 1945 with lobby support by the Mid-Continent Oil and Gas Association, an organization of large firms. To make the legislation politically palatable, the law required that 85 percent of the leases on a fully developed field approve unitization before the Corporation Commission could intervene. It also exempted from compulsory unitization all older fields discovered at least twenty years prior to the enactment of the law.

Immediately after passage of the compulsory unitization law, two major Oklahoma fields, West Edmond Hunton Lime and West Cement Medrano, were unitized by the Oklahoma Corporation Commission upon petition by the lease owners. Nevertheless, resistance by some firms to forced unitization on these fields led to unsuccessful efforts to repeal the compulsory unitization law in 1947 and a subsequent Oklahoma Supreme Court test (American Bar Association, 1949, p. 400). The intensity of the repeal efforts, which resulted in floor votes in both houses of the Oklahoma legislature, underscores the opposition of small firms to unitization, even though there were clear gains for the reservoirs involved. With unit management, output from the West Cement Medrano field increased by 70,000 barrels per day by 1951 by plugging wells with high gas/oil ratios to maintain subsurface pressure and by recycling natural gas back into the reservoir instead of selling it (Oklahoma Corporation Commission, West Cement Medrano Unit Files). By 1959, opposition to the Oklahoma compulsory unitization statute was largely spent, and the original law was amended with little controversy to lower the required majority for forced units from 85 to 63 percent (1951 Oklahoma Session Laws at 136).

In Texas, where small firms were even more numerous, successful opposition was mounted against the kinds of legislation adopted in Oklahoma, including wider well spacing, forced pooling of leases, and compulsory unitization. Available evidence suggests that in 1930 the average Texas producer was only 63 percent of the size of the average Oklahoma producer.[10] The difference in the incidence of small firms was exacerbated by the late 1930 discovery of East Texas field. Within three

[10]This excludes the ten largest firms in both states. Data are based on production reports in *Oil Weekly* (March 20, 1931). Comprehensive data were not available for Oklahoma for the very small firms, those with output less than $5,000, and those firms were not used in calculations.

years there were 1,000 primarily new firms on East Texas, three times as many as were reported for *all* of Oklahoma in 1930. Because of the influence of small producers on East Texas, state regulations to prorate production on that field were implemented only on a per well basis, whereas other Texas fields generally had prorating quotas based on 50 percent acreage and 50 percent wells.[11]

The benefits received by small firms on East Texas from this prorationing rule are reflected in their drilling practices. By 1933, small firms averaged one well per nine acres, whereas the twenty-four largest firms on the field averaged one well per fourteen acres. The Cole Committee of the U.S. House of Representatives, which was studying oil production practices, estimated that prorationing rules in East Texas contributed to the drilling of 23,000 unnecessary wells at a per well cost of $26,000 (U.S. House of Representatives, 1939, p. 503). Hence, existing prorationing regulation provided small East Texas operators with benefits and incentives to resist wide well spacing, lease pooling, and compulsory unitization.

Even when spacing laws were passed, widespread exemptions to spacing rules were granted by the Texas Railroad Commission to small producers, particularly on the East Texas field. The agency allowed all property owners access to the oil beneath their land in sufficient amounts to cover extraction costs. This regulatory practice promoted drainage and dense drilling. For example, a one-acre lot in Kilgore on the East Texas field had twenty-seven producing wells, and one-acre tracts with five to ten wells were common (American Bar Association, 1949, p. 493). Between 1938 and 1948, of the 100 well-spacing exemption cases heard by appellate courts in Texas, 99 concerned East Texas producers (American Bar Association, 1949, pp. 489–90). As late as 1959, the Railroad Commission did not establish well-spacing rules until eighteen months after the discovery of a new field. This delay, reflecting the political influence of small crude oil-producing firms, provided sufficient time to allow narrow well-spacing practices to become established (*Oil and Gas Journal,* May 1, 1959).

Both dense drilling and per well quotas provided small Texas firms with strategic advantages and a clear vested interest in prorationing regulation relative to unitization. Compulsory lease pooling was resisted by the Texas Independent Producers and Royalty Owners Association (TIPRO), an organization of small firms (*TIPRO Reporter,* February 1949). Compulsory pooling legislation did not pass the Texas legislature until 1965, twenty-four years after Oklahoma. Moreover TIPRO helped block changes in prorationing rules from a per well to an acreage basis

[11]The political problems faced by proponents of prorationing and the resulting policy concessions are outlined by Libecap and Wiggins (1984).

(*TIPRO Reporter*, September/October 1950). Preferential allocations to small lease owners continued through 1962, when per well quotas were overturned by the court in *Atlantic Refining Co. et al. v. Railroad Commission* (357 S.W.2d, 364 1962). TIPRO lobbied against compulsory unitization legislation, which has never been enacted in Texas. Under current law, unanimity voting rules are in force and voluntary, private units can be approved only after a field is fully developed. Hence, the early cost-saving unitization practiced on federal lands is impossible in Texas.

SUMMARY

The failure of unitization to be widespread, despite significant gains from unitizing oil production, is another example of how distributional conflicts over rental shares can limit the adoption of property rights to reduce common pool losses. Prorationing, as an alternative arrangement, has offered some relief from rent dissipation. Prorationing could be adopted because it allowed for side payments through favorable production quotas to politically influential parties that were not possible with unitization, even though unitization offered larger aggregate returns. These issues of the adoption of seemingly incomplete property rights arrangements are summarized in Chapter 7.

7

Concluding remarks

This volume joins a growing literature on institutional analysis by examining how particular property rights emerge or are modified. The gains from reducing common pool losses through the structure of property rights provide important incentives for institutional change. Common pool losses span those associated with classic open access resources, where no formal property rights exist and informal arrangements pose only limited constraints on behavior, to cases where formally defined property rights already are in place, but are too incomplete to prevent wasteful production practices. Although both existing informal property rules agreed to by the relevant parties or more formal, codified rights may be sufficient to channel behavior toward socially productive use of valuable resources, these status quo equilibria can be upset by changes in relative prices. Price changes through shifts in demand or supply conditions can generate greater competitive pressures for assets and thereby reduce ownership security. Depending on its extent, greater insecurity will lower time horizons in production decisions, reduce investment, and encourage too rapid exploitation.

Although the focus of the analysis has been on the political contracting behind four efforts to devise or to change property rights to natural resources in the United States, the implications of these studies can be applied to the broader examination of property rights institutions. In each of the cases, political bargaining involved both informal negotiations among claimants to devise local rules for resource use and lobbying to influence politicians and bureaucrats in legislation, court rulings, and administrative regulations regarding property rights. Despite the fact that bargaining involved similar natural resources and took place in a legal environment in the United States, which is generally favorable toward private property rights, the institutions adopted are surprisingly different, with distinct contracting histories and records of success in addressing common pool losses. Gaining a better understanding of this diversity and drawing implications for other settings is the goal of this volume.

The key for understanding the observed variation in property rights institutions is recognizing that the property rights that are devised to reduce the wastes of the common pool simultaneously define a distribution of wealth and political power. The record shows that in three of the four cases examined here few quarreled over the desirability of institutional change to promote more rational resource use and, hence, greater economic growth. Conflicts that developed arose over the distribution of property rights. Among bargaining parties, agreement on a proposed adjustment in property rights depends upon a favorable calculation of expected net private benefits under the new arrangement relative to status quo returns. Even then, parties have incentives to push for as large a share under the new arrangement as possible.

Attempts to reach a political consensus on changes in property rights involve negotiating side payments for influential parties by modifying the proposed rights structure. Those modifications, however, critically change the timing of institutional change, the nature of the institutions that ultimately are adopted, and the social gains that can be achieved. Because of the need to resolve the competing demands of various constituencies so that at least the most influential have a stake in the proposed change, the new property rights are likely to involve many compromises and bring only marginal adjustments from status quo conditions. Moreover, these changes in property rights generally will come late, when common pool losses and, hence, the gains from agreeement are large enough to facilitate side payments and other political exchanges to build a consensus for the new institutions. In short, institutional change is incremental, and the process of institutional change has an important impact on the result.

The empirical cases examined in the volume suggest that there is an important historical path dependence in determining the kind of property rights that can be adopted at any time. Past political agreements on property institutions create the framework for responding to new common pool losses, the identities of the agents for and opponents of change, their effectiveness in political bargaining, and the range of feasible alternatives. How constraining past arrangements are for institutional change is an empirical issue, which depends on the conditions surrounding each case. Nevertheless, the important role of history complicates the development of a theory to predict the timing, form, and impact of institutional change. The cases examined in this volume point out, however, that a theory that does not take into account prevailing distributional norms, past political agreements, the precedents they foster, and the vested interests they create will provide little insight into the process of institutional change.

Concluding Remarks

The four property rights cases that were analyzed can be placed into two similar groups:

1. Bargaining to devise local property rules and to obtain formal federal government recognition of private claims to federal mineral, timber, and range land.
2. Private and governmental efforts for controls on access to and production from fisheries and crude oil reservoirs.

A summary of these four cases reemphasizes some of the general patterns identified in the process of institutional change.

Although the federal land resource in the first group of cases was similar, the political contracting results were not. For private mineral rights, negotiations among miners in mining camps to establish rules for staking and enforcing claims and the later incorporation of those informal arrangements by state court rulings and statutes and by federal law occurred quickly with little controversy. The property rights structure that emerged reduced uncertainty, encouraged investment in mining, and promoted overall economic development in the Far West.

In terms of the analytical framework outlined in Chapter 2, there were several reasons for the speedy development of secure private mineral rights after the discovery of rich ore deposits in the West. First, there was broad agreement that the aggregate gains of institutional change were large. There was little dispute among even the earliest miners that some arrangement to divide and to protect private claims was necessary in order to realize the promised gold and silver bonanzas. Particularly after the most superficial deposits were taken, mining required that labor and capital be devoted to gaining access and processing the ore rather than in surveillance and predatory activities, that investment be made in costly tunnels and refining mills, and that mineral claims be exchanged from those who were skilled in prospecting to those who had advantages in raising capital and managing large-scale production.

Second, the miners who bargained in the mining camps for earliest rules were limited in number and were relatively homogeneous. Moreover, there were no critical other vested interest groups whose demands had to be met in assigning private mineral rights to federal land. Ore discoveries were in unclaimed areas, outside the path of agricultural settlement, which was the focus of general U.S. land policy. Third, the initial division among small claimants was within established distributional precedents for allocating federal lands. Fourth, because of the limited number of parties involved and inflated beliefs regarding the size of the ore discoveries, all parties expected to share in the benefits of a new institutional structure that guaranteed private mineral rights.

Finally, there were no acute information asymmetries regarding the valuing of individual claims to complicate the assignment of shares.

The second case in this group addressed the question of why federal land laws were not modified to recognize the prior appropriation claims of ranchers and timber companies as the law had been to incorporate the demands of miners earlier in the nineteenth century. As with mining, the intitial allocations especially for range land, were through informal agreements among ranchers who claimed acreage far in excess of the 160 acres allowed by federal land laws. For lumber companies, private arrangements were made with agents and entrymen to secure tracts of timber land through the fraudulent use of the land laws. As settlement progressed into the range and timber lands of the western United States and competition for the remaining unpatened land increased, these informal allocations became less secure, and ranchers, particularly, appealed to the federal government for formal recognition of their holdings through revision of the federal land laws. Unlike mining, however, efforts to provide mechanisms for obtaining secure private tenure to federal timber and range lands were much less successful.

Lobbying of congressional politicians and of officials in the General Land Office to allow for larger claims than the 160 acres allowed by law and for recognition of commercial timber claims on land that was generally unsuitable for agriculture brought only minimal and late responses. Even though the 1879 Public Lands Commission had called for 2,560-acre homesteads and cash sales of other federal land, no action was taken except for the 1909 and 1916 revisions of the Homestead Act, which relaxed the acreage constraints to 320 and 640 acres in certain areas.

The proposed changes in federal land law for range and timber land were politically controversial and were rejected by politicians and bureaucratic agencies for several reasons. First, the aggregate gains from revising the land laws were disputed. Although fraud was a very costly way of obtaining federal timber land, it was condemned by politicians because it was used by large lumber companies, not because it was costly. It appears that where fraud was used by homesteaders to gain additional range or farm land beyond the 160 acres allowed by law, politicians were much less concerned (Libecap, 1981a, p. 34). Any costs of overgrazing of range land from the failure to respond quickly to the lack of secure tenure were cumulative with less immediate political impact, and the extent of overharvest of timber was likely to have been small at the time. The claims by ranchers that acreage greater than 160 acres was needed for successful ranching and farming also were challenged. There were virgin grass stands to be exploited and strongly held beliefs that dryland farming techniques could be adopted quite easily by homesteaders. Many timber lands also were held to have agricultural potential. Hence, it appeared to politicians and administrators in the General Land Office that an alternative distribution of land to homesteaders was a viable possibility.

Second, the number of bargaining parties involved in changing federal land laws was large and heterogeneous. The precedent of federal land law for an egalitarian distribution of land to small farmers established expectations for and vested interests in the allocation of the remaining stock of federal land, which was declining by the end of the nineteenth century. With the large number of past and potential homestead claimants, related commercial interests, and the existence of the General Land Office as an established administrative agency for the piecemeal allocation of federal land, there were strong political pressures on Congress to reject the land claims of ranchers and timber companies. The relative lobby influence of ranchers may have been further weakened by disputes among cattle and sheep raisers.

Third, the proposed division of land requested by ranchers and timber companies appeared to violate the distributional norms reflected in the federal land laws. Because there was no agreement that the informal claims of ranchers or the proposed land acquisitions of timber companies had legal standing, political side payment schemes to compensate them or to facilitate trades with homesteaders could not be devised.

In the second group of cases, similar contracting problems were encountered in attempts to devise secure rights to harvest fish and to extract crude oil. In both instances, institutional changes in response to common pool problems have occurred late, after many of the social costs had been borne, and even then only limited adjustments from status quo conditions have been enacted.

In fisheries and crude oil production in the United States there generally has been a consensus on the aggregate costs of common pool production. At issue though, has been the type of property rights arrangement that can be adopted to reduce those losses. In both cases, legal precedents and existing regulatory policies have limited the range of feasible contracting options. The legal environment includes the common law rule of capture, which governs the assignment of property rights to both fish and oil; the prohibition of private property rights to most fish stocks; the retention of mineral rights to subsurface oil by surface landowners; and regulatory practices, such as guarantees of the freedom to fish for most citizens and prorationing of oil production among producing wells. Through its allocation of property rights, this legal environment had created an array of stakeholders who have a vested interest in the status quo and whose demands must be considered in any proposed institutional change.

By most measures common pool losses in U.S. fisheries and crude oil reservoirs have been large. Many fisheries are characterized by overharvest, excessive capitalization, redundant labor, low incomes, and, for some, the biological depletion of species. Because of the political rejection of private property rights, efforts to control fishing have focused on government regulatory policies to limit harvest or to augment stocks. In many cases though, these regulatory efforts appear to have been excessively costly and have left many margins open for continued rent dissipation.

Similarly, crude oil production historically has been characterized by too rapid extraction rates, overcapitalization, and reduced oil recovery. The most complete solution to the common pool problem in oil production, unitization, has been difficult to implement privately in a timely manner. Government policy, reflecting, in part, the political opposition to forced unitization, has relied largely on prorationing, whereby production quotas are assigned to individual wells. Prorationing, though, has brought only limited gains relative to those possible under unitization. With the incentive to drill that has existed under prorationing rules, as late as 1980, the United States had 88 percent of the world's oil wells, but only 14 percent of the world's oil production (*International Petroleum Encyclopedia,* 1982, pp. 334–5).

The contracting problem in devising more effective institutional responses to common pool losses in fisheries and in crude oil production has centered on the distribution of the resource rents. Distributional conflicts have been exacerbated by heterogeneities among the bargaining parties with fishermen varying according to skill, equipment, size, and type of fish caught and with oil companies varying according to size and value of oil leases, among other factors. These differences have made private agreement on share allocations exceedingly difficult, and they have hindered the formation of cohesive lobby groups to influence the actions of politicians and bureaucrats in devising regulations and more formal property rights. Further, some fishermen and oil companies have adjusted well to and benefit from status quo conditions. They are concerned that proposed regulations to more tightly restrict output through greater controls on access and individual production will reduce their share of fishery or oil reservoir rents. Information problems regarding catch histories, oil lease values, and the reaction of fish stocks and oil reservoirs to regulatory change add to the problem of developing a share formula that will make critical parties better off in negotiations for unitization or fishery regulations.

Distributional conflicts present political risks to politicians, giving them incentives to propose regulations that do not seriously upset status quo rankings and that offer only limited relief from common pool losses, such as oil production prorationing or restricted seasons for fishing. Similar incentives exist for regulatory agencies that have a vested interest in maintaining and expanding regulatory authority, a goal that is likely to be inconsistent with the establishment of more secure private property rights.

In conclusion, the analysis presented in this volume suggests that swift institutional responses to common pool losses to promote more rational resource use and greater economic growth cannot be taken for granted. Distributional conflicts inherent in any new property rights arrangement, even one that offers important efficiency implications, can block or critically constrain the institutions that can be adopted. By compensating those potentially harmed in the proposed definition of rights, a political consensus for institutional change may emerge. Those share concesssions, however, necessarily alter the nature of the rights that are adopted and the size of the gains that are possible. More attention accordingly, must be directed to the distributional implications of property rights arrangements, to the identity and preferences of the various bargaining parties, to the nature of the side payment schemes adopted, and, importantly, to the history of past political agreements, if the observed variations in property rights and associated economic behavior are to be understood.

References

Acheson, J. M. "The Lobster Fiefs: Economic and Ecological Effects of Territoriality in the Maine Lobster Industry." *Human Ecology* No. 3 (1975): 183–207.

Adelman, M. A. "Efficiency of Resource Use in Crude Petroleum." *Southern Economic Journal* 31 (1964):101–22.

Agnello, R. J., and Donnelley, L. P. "Property Rights and Efficiency in the Oyster Industry." *Journal of Law and Economics* 18 (1975):521–34.

Ahlstrom, E. H., and Radovich, J. "Management of the Pacific Sardine." In *A Century of Fisheries in North America,* edited by N. G. Bensen. Special Publication 7, 183–84. Washington, D.C.: American Fisheries Society, 1970.

Alchian, A. A., and Demsetz, H. "Production, Information Costs, and Economic Organization." *American Economic Review,* 62 (1972):777–95.

———. "Property Rights Paradigm." *Journal of Economic History* 33 (1973): 16–27.

American Bar Association. *Legal History of Conservation of Oil and Gas.* Chicago: American Bar Association, 1938.

———. *Conservation of Oil and Gas: A Legal History.* Chicago: American Bar Association, 1949.

American Institute of Mining and Metallurgical Engineers. *Transactions of the AIME* 86 (1930:11–21.

American Petroleum Institute. *Petroleum Facts and Figures.* Washington, D.C.: American Petroleum Institute, 1951.

Andersen, R. "Public and Private Access Management in Newfoundland Fishing." In *North Atlantic Maritime Cultures: Anthropological Essays on Changing Adaptions,* edited by R. Andersen, 299–336. New York: Mouton Publishers, 1979.

Andersen, R., and Stiles, R. G. "Resources Management and Spatial Competition in Newfoundland Fishing: An Exploratory Essay." In *Seafarer and Community,* edited by P. H. Frickle, 44–66. London: Croom Helm, 1973.

Anderson, T. L., and Hill, P. J. "The Evolution of Property Rights: A Study of the American West. *Journal of Law and Economics* 18 (1975):163–79.

Bain, J. S. *The Economics of the Pacific Coast Petroleum Industry, Part III: Public Policy Toward Competition and Prices.* Berkeley: University of California Press, 1947.

Barnes, W. C., and Jardine, J. T. *Meat Situation in the U.S.,* Part II, *Livestock Production in the Eleven Far Western Range States. U.S. Department of*

Agriculture Report no. 110. Washington, D.C.: U.S. Government Printing Office, 1916.

Barnett, H. J., and Morse C. *Scarcity and Growth: The Economics of Natural Resource Availability.* Baltimore, Md.: Johns Hopkins University Press, 1963.

Barzel, Y. "The Entrepreneur's Reward for Self-Policying." *Economic Inquiry* 25 (1987):103–16.

Bell, F. W. "Technological Externalities and Common-Property Resources: An Empirical Study of the U.S. Northern Lobster Fishery." *Journal of Political Economy* 80 (1972):148–58.

Binger, B. R., and Hoffman, E. "Institutions as Public Goods: The Question of Efficiency." *Journal of Theoretical and Institutional Economics.* 145 (1989):67–84.

Breton, Y. D. "The Influence of Modernization on the Modes of Production in Coastal Fishing: An Example From Venezuela." *Those Who Live From the Sea,* edited by M. E. Smith, 125–38. New York: West Publishing Company, 1977.

Buchanan, J. M., Tollison, R., and Tullock, G. (eds.). *Towards a Theory of the Rent-Seeking Society.* College Station: Texas A&M University Press, 1981.

Buchanan, J. M., and Tullock, G. *The Calculus of Consent.* Ann Arbor: University of Michigan Press, 1962.

Cheung, S. N. S. "The Structure of a Contract and the Theory of a Non-Exclusive Resource." *Journal of Law and Economics* 13 (1970):49–70.

Coase, R. H. "The Nature of the Firm." *Economical* 4 (1937):386–405.

———. "The Problem of Social Cost." *Journal of Law and Economics* 3 (1960):1–44.

Copp, H. N. *Public Land Laws.* Washington, D.C.: U.S. Government Printing Office, 1883.

Cordell, J. "Carrying Capacity Analysis of Fixed-Territorial Fishing." *Ethnology* 17 (1978):1–24.

Danhof, C. H. "Farm-Making Costs and the 'Safety Valve': 1850–60." *Journal of Political Economy* 49 (1941):317–59.

Davis, L. E., and North, D. C. *Institutional Change and American Economic Growth.* Cambridge, England: Cambridge University Press, 1971.

De Alessi, L. "The Economics of Property Rights: A Review of the Evidence." *Research in Law and Economics* 2 (1980):1–47.

Demsetz, H. "Towards a Theory of Property Rights," *American Economic Review* 57 (1967):347–59.

Dennen, R. T. "Cattlemen's Associations and Property Rights in Land in the American West." *Explorations in Economic History* 13 (1976):423–36.

Donaldson, T. *The Public Domain: Its History With Statistics.* 47th Congr., 2d sess., House Miscellaneous Document 45, Part 4. Washington, D.C.: U.S. Government Printing Office, 1884.

Federal Oil Conservation Board. *Complete Record of Public Hearings.* Washington, D.C.: U.S. Government Printing Office, 1926.

———. *Report III.* Washington, D.C.: U.S. Government Printing Office, 1929.

Fernow, B. E. *Economics of Forestry: A Reference Book for Students of Political Economy and Professional and Lay Students of Forestry.* New York: Thomas Y. Crowell Co, 1902.

Field, B. "The Optimal Commons." *American Journal of Agricultural Economics* 67 (1985):364–7.

Forman, S. "Cognition and the Catch: The Location of Fishing Spots in a Brazilian Coastal Village." *Ethnology* 6 (1967):417–26.
Friedman, L. M. *A History of American Law.* 2d ed. New York: Simon & "Schuster, 1985.
Furubotn, E. G., and Pejovich, S. "Property Rights and Economic Theory: A Survey of Recent Literature." *Journal of Economic Literature* 10 (1972):1137–62.
Gates, P. W. *History of Public Land Law Development.* Washington, D.C.: Public Land Law Review Commission, 1968.
———. "Pressure Groups and Recent American Land Policies." *Agricultural History* 55 (1981): 103–27.
Goldberg, V. P. "Regulation and Administered Contracts." *Bell Journal of Economics* 7 (1976):426–48.
Gordon, H. S. "The Economic Theory of a Common Property Resource: The Fishery." *Journal of Political Economy* 62 (1954):124–42.
Hallagan, W. S. "Share Contracting for California Gold." *Explorations in Economic History* 15 (1978):196–210.
Hargreaves, M. W. *Dry Farming in the Northern Great Plains, 1900–1925.* Cambridge: Harvard University Press, 1957.
Hays, S. *Conservation and the Gospel of Efficiency: The Progressive Conservation Movement, 1890–1920.* Cambridge: Harvard University Press, 1959.
Hibbard, B. H. *History of Public Land Policies.* New York: Macmillan, 1924.
Hidy, R., Hill, F., and Nevins, A. *Timber and Men: The Weyerhaeuser Story.* New York: Macmillan, 1963.
Higgs, R. "Legally Induced Technical Regress in the Washington Salmon Fishery." *Research in Economic History* 7 (1982)55–86.
Hoffman, E., and Spitzer, M. L. "Entitlements, Rights, and Fairness: An Experimental Examination of Subjects' Concepts of Distributive Justice." *Journal of Legal Studies* 14 (1985):259–98.
Hughes, J. R. T. *The Governmental Habit.* New York: Basic Books, 1977.
Hurst, J. W. *Law and Social Process in the United States History.* Ann Arbor: University of Michigan Law School, 1960.
———. *Law and Economic Growth: The Legal History of the Lumber Industry in Wisconsin, 1836–1915.* Cambridge: Harvard University Press, 1964.
International Petroleum Encyclopedia (1982). Tulsa: Penn Well.
Isaac, R. M., and Reynolds, S. S. "Innovation and Property Rights in Information: An Experimental Approach to Testing Hypotheses About Private R&D Behavior." In *Advances in the Study of Entrepreneurship, Innovation, and Economic Growth,* edited by G. D. Libecap, Vol. 1. Greenwich, Conn.: JAI Press, 1986:129–156.
Ise, J. *The United States Oil Policy.* New Haven, Conn.: Yale University Press, 1926.
Jensen, M. C., and Meckling, W. H. "Theory of the Firm: Managerial Behavior, Agency Costs, and Ownership Structure." *Journal of Financial Economics* 3 (1976):305–60.
Johnson, R. N. "U. S. Forest Service Policy and Its Budget." In *Forest Lands: Public and Private,* edited by R. T. Deacon and M. B. Johnson. Cambridge: Ballenger, 103–132.
Johnson, R. N., and Libecap, G. D. "Efficient Markets and Great Lakes Timber: A Conservation Issue Reexamined." *Explorations in Economic History* 17 (1980a):372–85.

———. "Agency Costs and the Assignment Property Rights: The Case of Southwestern Indian Reservations." *Southern Economic Journal* 47 (1980b):332–47.

———. "Contracting Problems and Regulations: The Case of the Fishery." *American Economic Review* 72 (1982):1005–22.

———. "Agency Growth, Salaries and the Protected Bureaucrat." *Economic Inquiry,* in press.

Journal of the Council of the First Legislative Assembly of the Territory of Nevada. San Francisco: Valentine and Co, 1862.

Laws of the Territory of Nevada, First Session, San Francisco: Valentine and Company, 1862.

Laws of the Territory of Nevada, Second Session, Virginia City, Nevada: Goodman and Company, 1863.

Libecap, G. D. "Economic Variables and the Development of the Law: The Case of Western Mineral Rights." *Journal of Economic History* 38 (1978a):338–62.

———. *The Evolution of Private Mineral Rights: Nevada's Comstock Lode.* New York: Arno Press, 1978b.

———. "Government Support of Private Claims to Public Minerals: Western Mineral Rights." *Business History Review,* 53 (1979):364–85.

———. *Locking Up the Range: Federal Land Controls and Grazing.* Cambridge: Ballinger, 1981a.

———. "Bureaucratic Opposition to the Assignment of Property Rights: Overgrazing on the Western Range." *Journal of Economic History* 41 (1981b):151–8.

———. "The Political Allocation of Mineral Rights: A Reevaluation of Teapot Dome." *Journal of Economic History* 44 (1984):381–91.

———. "Property Rights in Economic History: Implications for Research." *Explorations in Economic History* 23 (1986): 227–52.

Libecap, G. D., and Johnson, R. N. "Property Rights, Nineteenth-Century Federal Timber Policy, and the Conservation Movement." *Journal of Economic History* 39 (1979):129–42.

———. "Legislating Commons: The Navajo Tribal Council and the Navajo Range." *Economic Inquiry* 18 (1980):69–86.

Libecap, G. D., and Wiggins, S. N. "Contractual Responses to the Common Pool: Prorationing of Crude Oil Production." *American Economic Review* 74 (1984):87–98.

———. "The Influence of Private Contractual Failure on Regulation: The Case of Oil Field Unitization." *Journal of Political Economy* 93 (1985):690–714.

Lord, E. *Comstock Mining and Miners,* U. S. Geological Survey Monographs, Vol. IV. Washington, D.C.: U.S. Government Printing Office, 1882.

Lund, T. A. *American Wildlife Law.* Berkeley: University of California Press, 1980.

Marsh, A. J. *Official Report of the Debates and Proceedings in the Constitutional Convention of the State of Nevada.* San Francisco: Frank Eastman, 1866.

Martin, K. O. "Play by the Rules or Don't Play at All: Space Division and Resource Allocation in a Rural Newfoundland Fishing Community." In *North Atlantic Maritime Cultures: Anthropological Essays on Changing Adaptations,* edited by R. Andersen, 277–98. New York: Mounton Publishers, 1979.

McCloskey, D. N. "The Enclosure of Open Fields: Preface to a Study of Its

Impact on the Efficiency of English Agriculture in the Eighteenth Century." *Journal of Economic History* 32 (1972):15–35.
McCurdy, C. W. "Stephen J. Field and Public Land Law Development in California, 1850–1866: A Case Study of Judicial Resource Allocation in Nineteenth Century America." *Law and Society Review* 10 (1976):235–66.
McEvoy, A. F. *The Fishermen's Problems: Ecology and Law in The California Fisheries, 1950–1980.* New York: Cambridge University Press, Studies in Environment and History, 1986.
Myers, R. M. *The Law of Pooling and Unitization: Voluntary, Compulsory,* 2d ed. Albany, N.Y.: Banks and Co, 1957.
North, D. C. "Structure and Performance: The Task of Economic History." *Journal of Economic Literature* 16 (1978):963–78.
———. *Structure and Change in Economic History.* New York: Norton, 1981.
North, D. C., and Thomas, R. P. *The Rise of the Western World: A New Economic History.* Cambridge, England: Cambridge University Press, 1973.
Olson, M. *The Logic of Collective Action.* Cambridge: Harvard University Press, 1965.
———. *The Rise and Decline of Nations.* New Haven, Conn.: Yale University Press, 1982.
Olson, S. H. *The Depletion Myth: A History of Railroad Use of Timber.* Cambridge: Harvard University Press, 1961.
Osgood, E. S. *The Day of the Cattleman.* Minneapolis: University of Minnesota Press, 1929.
Parr, V. V., Collier, G. W., and Klemmendson, G. S. *Ranch Organization and Methods of Livestock Production in the Southwest.* U. S. Department of Agriculture, Technical Bulletin no. 68. Washington, D. C.: U. S. Government Printing Officer, 1928.
Peffer, E. L. *The Closing of the Public Domain: Disposal and Reservation Policies, 1900–50.* Stanford: Stanford University Press, 1951.
Peltzman, S. "Toward a More General Theory of Regulation." *Journal of Law and Economics* 19 (1976): 211–40.
Puter, S. A. D. *Looters of the Public Domain.* Portland, Oregon: Portland Printing House, 1908.
Report of the Auditor of the Territory of Nevada, Virginia City, Nevada: John Church State Printer, 1864.
Robbins, R. M. *Our Landed Heritage: The Public Domain, 1776–1970.* 2d ed. Lincoln, Nebraska: University of Nebraska Press, 1976.
Scheiber, H. N. *Ohio Canal Era: A Case Study of Government and the Economy 1820–1861.* Athens: Ohio University Press, 1969.
———. "Property Law, Expropriation, and Resource Allocation by Government: The United States, 1789–1910." *Journal of Economic History* 33 (1973):232–51.
———. "Regulation, Property Rights, and Definition of 'The Market': Law and the American Economy." *Journal of Economic History* 41 (1981):103–9.
Scott, A. "The Fishery: The Objectives of Sole Ownership." *Journal of Political Economy* 63 (1955):116–24.
———. "Development of Economic Theory on Fisheries Regulation." *Journal of the Fishery Research Board of Canada* 36 (1979):725–41.
———. "The Conceptual Origins of Rights-Based Fishing." Paper presented to the NATO Advanced Research Workshop, Reykjavik, Iceland, July 1988.

Shannon, F. A. "A Post Mortem on the Labor-Safety-Valve Theory." *Agricultural History* 19 (1945):31–8.
Shinn, C. H. *Mining Camps, A Study in American Frontier Government.* New York: Alfred A. Knopf, 1948.
Steer, H. B. *Stumpage Prices of Privately Owned Timber in the United States.* U.S. Department of Agriculture, Technical Bulletin no. 626. Washington, D.C.: U. S. Government Printing Office, 1938.
Stigler, G. "The Theory of Economic Regulation." *Bell Journal of Economics* 2 (1971):3–21.
Stockslager, S. M. *Cattle Graziers on Public Lands.* House Executive Document no. 232, 50th Congr., 1st sess. Washington, D.C.: U. S. Government Printing Office, 1888.
Taylor, H. M. "Condition of the Cattle-Range Industry." In *Annual Report,* Bureau of Animal Industry, U. S. Department of Agriculture, 105–24). Washington, D.C.: U.S. Government Printing Office, 1886.
Tober, J. A. *Who Owns the Wildlife? The Political Economy of Conservation in Nineteenth Century America.* Contributions in Economics and Economic History no. 37. Westport, Conn.: Greenwood Press, 1981.
Transcript of Record. *Gulf Coast Shrimpers and Oystermen's Association v. United States.* no. 15680, 5th Circuit, U. S. Court of Appeals, 1956.
Turner, F. J. *The Frontier in American History.* New York: Holt, Rinehart & Winston, 1962.
Umbeck, J. "The California Gold Rush: A Study of Emerging Property Rights." *Explorations in Economic History* 14 (1977):197–226.
———. "A Theory of Contract Choice and the California Gold Rush." *The Journal of Law and Economics* 20 (1977b):421–37.
———. "Might Makes Right: A Theory of the Foundation and Initial Distribution of Property Rights." *Economic Inquiry* 19 (1981):38–59.
U. S. Department of Agriculture. *The Western Range.* 74th Congr., 2d sess., Senate Document 199. Washington, D.C.: U.S. Government Printing Office, 1936.
U. S. Department of Commerce, Bureau of the Census. *Historical Statistics of the United States Colonial Times to 1970.* Washington, D.C.: U. S. Government Printing Office, 1975.
———. *Fishery Statistics of the United States,* Washington, D.C.: U. S. Government Printing Office, 1977.
U. S. Department of the Interior. *Report of the Commissioner of the General Land Office.* Washington, D.C.: U.S. Government Printing Office, 1868.
———. *Report of the Commissioner of the General Land Office.* Washington, D.C.: U.S. Government Printing Office, 1874.
———. *Report of the Commissioner of the General Land Office.* Washington, D.C.: U.S. Government Printing Office, 1875.
———. *Report of the Commissioner of the General Land Office.* Washington, D.C.: U.S. Government Printing Office, 1886.
———. *Report of the Commissioner of the General Land Office.* Washington, D.C.: U.S. Government Printing Office, 1897.
———. *Report of the Commissioner of the General Land Office.* Washington, D.C.: U.S. Government Printing Office, 1913.
———. *Annual Report of the Secretary.* Washington, D.C.: U. S. Government Printing Office, 1902.

U. S. Department of the Interior, Bureau of the Census. *Compendium of the Eleventh Census, 1890.* Part I. Washington, D.C.: U. S. Government Printing Office, 1892.

———. *Abstract of the Eleventh Census, 1890.* Washington, D.C.: U. S. Government Printing Office, 1894.

U. S. Department of the Treasury. *Report of the Director of the Mint.* Washington, D.C.: U. S. Government Printing Office, 1881.

———. *Report of the Director of the Mint.* Washington, D.C.: U.S. Government Printing Office, 1891.

U. S. House of Representatives. *Statistics of Mines and Mining in the States and Territories West of the Rocky Mountains.* Executive Document 177, 43rd Congr., 2d sess. Washington, D.C.: U. S. Government Printing Office, 1874.

———. *Report of the Public Lands Commission.* House Executive Document no. 46, 46th Congr., 2d sess. Washington, D.C.: U. S. Government Printing Office, 1880.

———. "Hearing on House Resolution 290 and HR 7372 to Promote the Conservation of Petroleum; to Provide for Cooperation with the States in Preventing Waste of Petroleum; to Create an Office of Petroleum Conservation." Cole Committee, 76th Congr. Washington, D.C.: U. S. Government Printing Office, 1939.

U. S. Senate. *Unauthorized Fencing of Public Lands.* Executive Document no. 127, 48th Congr., 2st sess. Washington, D.C.: U.S. Government Printing Office, 1884.

———. *Report of the Public Lands Commission.* Senate Document no. 189, 58th Congr., 3d sess. Washington, D.C.: U. S. Government Printing Office, 1905.

Weingast, B. R., and Moran, M. J. "Bureaucratic Discretion or Congressional Control? Regulatory Policy Making by the Federal Trade Commission." *Journal of Political Economy* 91 (1983):765–800.

Wiggins, S. N., and Libecap, G. D. "Oil Field Unitization: Contractual Failure in the Presence of Imperfect Information." *American Economic Review* 75 (1985):368–85.

Williams, H. R. "Conservation of Oil and Gas." *Harvard Law Review* 65 (1952):1115–84.

Williamson, O. E. "Franchise Bidding for Natural Monopolies—In General and with Respect to CATV." *Bell Journal of Economics* 7 (1976):73–104.

———. "The Modern Corporation: Origins, Evolution, Attributes." *Journal of Economic Literature* 19 (1981):1537–68.

Wilson, James A. "A Test of the Tragedy of the Commons" in *Managing the Commons,* edited by Garrett Harden and John Baden, San Francisco: W. H. Freeman and Co. 1977:96–100.

Wooten, E. O. *Factors Affecting Range Management in New Mexico.* U. S. Department of Agriculture, Bulletin no. 211. Washington, D.C.: U. S. Government Printing Office, 1915.

———. *The Relation of Land Tenure to the Use of the Arid Grazing Lands of the Southwestern States.* U. S. Department of Agriculture, Bulletin no. 1001. Washington, D.C.: U. S. Government Printing Office, 1922.

Index

Index